The United States and The World Economy

Other Titles Published in Cooperation with the Center for Strategic and International Studies, Georgetown University

†*International Security Yearbook 1984/85,* edited by Barry M. Blechman and Edward N. Luttwak

NATO: The Next Generation, Robert E. Hunter

Bioenergy and Economic Development: Planning for Biomass Energy Programs in the Third World, William Ramsay

Modern Weapons and Third World Powers, Rodney W. Jones and Steven A. Hildreth

The Emerging Pacific Community, edited by Robert L. Downen and Bruce J. Dickson

The Cuban Revolution: 25 Years Later, Hugh S. Thomas, Georges A. Fauriol, and Juan Carlos Weiss

Banks, Petrodollars, and Sovereign Debtors, Penelope Hartland-Thunberg

Forecasting U.S. Electricity Demand: Trends and Methodologies, Adela Bolet

U.S.-Japanese Energy Relations: Cooperation and Competition, edited by Charles K. Ebinger and Ronald A. Morse

National Security and Strategic Minerals: An Analysis of U.S. Dependence on Foreign Sources of Cobalt, Barry M. Blechman

†Available in hardcover and paperback.

About the Book

The structure of the world economy has changed dramatically in recent years, reflecting a redefinition of U.S. interests in light of increasing foreign penetration in U.S. markets, global pressures for protectionist policies, the emergence of the newly industrializing countries, and the vulnerabilities of the international financial system. This collection of essays addresses these and other developments facing policymakers in business, government, and labor. The authors discuss policy challenges in international trade, technological competition, exchange-rate disequilibrium, Third World debt, and the role of the private sector.

PUBLISHED IN COOPERATION WITH
THE CENTER FOR STRATEGIC AND INTERNATIONAL STUDIES
GEORGETOWN UNIVERSITY

The United States and The World Economy: Policy Alternatives for New Realities

edited by
John N. Yochelson
with the assistance of
Catherine Stirling

Westview Press / Boulder and London

Copyright © 1985 by The Center for Strategic and International Studies, Georgetown University

Published in 1985 in the United States of America by Westview Press, Inc., 5500 Central Avenue, Boulder, Colorado 80301; Frederick A. Praeger, Publisher

Library of Congress Cataloging in Publication Data
Main entry under title:
The U.S. and the world economy.
   (A Westview special study)
   1. United States—Commercial policy—Addresses, essays, lectures. I. Yochelson, John N. II. Title:
The U.S. and the world economy.
HF1455.U143   1985   337.73   85-3298
ISBN 0-8133-7003-5

Composition for this book was provided by CSIS
Printed and bound in the United States of America

10   9   8   7   6   5   4   3   2

Contents

About the Authors

Jonathan D. Aronson is an associate professor of international relations at the University of Southern California. He recently completed a Council on Foreign Relations International Affairs fellowship in the Office of the U.S. Trade Representative.

Paul R. Krugman is the Ford Associate Professor of International Business Management and Economics at the Sloan School of Management of the Massachusetts Institute of Technology. He spent 1982-1983 on leave as an international policy economist at the Council of Economic Advisers.

Harald B. Malmgren is the president of Malmgren, Inc. and is an adjunct professor at the School of Foreign Service, Georgetown University. He also has served as Deputy Special Trade Representative at the Office of the U.S. Trade Representative.

Stephen A. Merrill is a fellow and director of Technology and International Business Studies at the Center. Previously he was on the professional staff of the Senate Commerce, Science and Transportation Committee.

Gordon Richards is director of economic analysis at the National Association of Manufacturers. In 1983 he received his Ph.D. in political science from the University of Chicago.

John N. Yochelson is the director of the CSIS International Business and Economics program and the Quadrangular Forum. He previously served with the State Department and as a consultant to the Joint Economic Committee of the Congress.

Foreword

One of the great strengths of the American political process is its capacity to draw upon the views and experience of those outside government. Thoughtful people from business, labor, and the policy research community have long been a rich resource for the executive branch and Congress. At their best, they bring not only practical insights and fresh ideas but that rarest of commodities in Washington—perspective beyond the day-to-day issues that often threaten to overwhelm policymakers.

Nowhere is the need for creative thinking more apparent than in the international economic arena. The world economy has been transformed over the past 15 years by the shift from the gold standard to floating exchange rates, the oil shocks of the 1970s, the explosive growth of Third World debt, the emergence of newly industrializing countries as world-class competitors, and the accelerating pace of technological change. These developments have made the challenges faced by the United States more demanding than ever. They have speeded the internationalization of the U.S. economy, creating new opportunities and vulnerabilities. As traditional lines between domestic and international policy agendas have blurred, the task of defining, integrating, and promoting U.S. interests has become all the more important.

In the early fall of 1982, the Center for Strategic and International Studies of Georgetown University proposed that I help form a working group of leading representatives from the business, labor, and policy research communities to examine the key challenges facing the United States and its major Western trading partners. Counterpart groups focusing on the same agenda were established in Canada, Europe, and Japan under the leadership of former Minister of Trade Edward Lumley, former Vice President of the European Communities Commission Etienne Davignon, and former Japanese Foreign Minister Saburo Okita respectively.

Together, these four groups constituted the Quadrangular Forum that has met regularly since the spring of 1983. The forum has produced some excellent policy papers, while at the same time concentrating its efforts on the annual economic summits of Western leaders as a timely opportunity to widen the dialogue between government officials and representatives of the private sector. The presummit meetings have been of great value to all who have participated.

This volume contains a selection of the most stimulating policy papers done by the American participants in the Quadrangular Forum. Harald Malmgren argues that the United States has entered an era of managed trade in which the challenge of keeping world markets open will be increasingly difficult. He raises a host of basic questions that must be addressed in thinking through U.S. interests in this new setting. John Yochelson analyzes the impact of U.S. economic resurgence on relations with our European and East Asian trading partners. He foresees a sustained period of assertiveness in U.S. economic diplomacy, driven partly by the commitment of the Reagan administration to market forces but also by the pressure of increasing trade deficits. Jonathan Aronson and Paul Krugman analyze the vital interrelationship between trade flows, exchange rates, and the management of international debt. They lay out options for adjusting the policy process, both domestically and internationally, to address these interrelationships more effectively. Stephen Merrill assesses technological competition among the advanced and industrializing countries. Merrill's perceptive analysis of U.S. vulnerabilities and assets in high technology advances the debate on industrial strategy. Gordon Richards compares two explanations of the forces that are driving the performance of the U.S. economy. He contends that shifting macroeconomic policy, more than structural factors, accounts for the key changes that have been taking place in the industrial sector.

All of us who have read and debated these essays have gained much from them. They deserve to be widely circulated. CSIS is to be highly commended for its fine work in illuminating the international economic issues that face the United States.

William E. Brock
The U.S. Trade Representative

Acknowledgments

All of the members of the Quadrangular Forum owe great thanks to Ambassador William E. Brock for his enthusiasm and leadership. I would also like to acknowledge the invaluable counsel of Geza Feketekuty, senior assistant U.S. trade representative, and Jim Frierson, special assistant to Ambassador Brock.

The papers within this volume benefited enormously from the editorial skills of my colleagues Penelope Hartland-Thunberg, Stephen Merrill, and especially Catherine Stirling. Pat Gaines typed the manuscript, and Andrew Gilmour and Rose Marie Goncz provided superb support for the American participants.

The Quadrangular Forum has been made possible by generous grants from the Dr. Scholl Foundation, the C. V. Starr Foundation, and the help of a broad range of corporate supporters.

John N. Yochelson
Spring 1985

Trade Policy and Trade Negotiations in the 1980s

by
Harald B. Malmgren

World trade was a powerful engine of growth from the end of World War II to the end of the 1970s, growing much faster than the GNP during that period. This rapid expansion of trade tied the economies of the industrialized Western free market nations more closely and drew the economies of the developed and developing nations into a more interactive and dynamic relationship.

Developing nations grew faster than the mature industrialized nations, and this brought about major shifts in the pattern of world demand. In the 1970s, the developing countries became the fastest growing markets for exports from the major trading nations. The share of total U.S. and European Common Market exports destined for Third World markets approached 40 percent, and more than half of all Japanese exports were sent to these developing countries' markets.

World trade also underwent a period of turbulence and structural change since the beginning of the 1970s. Profound shocks—inflation, abrupt energy price changes, exchange rate volatility, emergence of many new world class competitors, rapid international transfers of technology—put pressure on workers, farmers, and industries throughout the world. Investment in basic industries slowed down, because of flagging confidence, at the very time when investment should have been accelerated to cope with the new market realities.

The economic trauma that ensued generated pressures on all governments to act—and they did. Government intervention grew, even in the most advanced economies, through subsidies, protectionism, and other nationalistic measures. It is true that a fad for deregulation took hold in some countries, like the United States and the United Kingdom, but these liberalizing effects were overwhelmed by a world trend toward sectoral improvisation by governments. Virtually everywhere today governments are trying to boost exports, limit imports, and stimulate domestic job creation. This continuous improvisation has put more and more power in the hands of government officials. Given their inherent administrative latitude, more uncertainties have

1

been generated about the future conditions of competition. Such uncertainties themselves act as a further impediment to trade and investment flows.

Thus added to the economic shocks of the 1970s were new forces of disturbance and disruption generated by governments in their artificial efforts to enhance domestic and international competitiveness. In the early 1980s, the cumulative debt service pressures added further impetus to economic nationalism in developing countries. Moreover, the prolonged slowdown in world economic growth, and the virtual stagnation of world trade from 1979 to 1983, greatly increased pressures on all governments.

There also has been a strong tendency on the part of governments in each of the major industrialized nations to assert that they maintain the only free market, and that the unfair and even predatory policies of other nations are to blame for industrial and agricultural troubles. As a political response, in North American and West European nations, the concept of bilateral reciprocity has been brought back to life, like Count Dracula, to attack the troublemakers.

Added to these haphazard forces is the growing role of the non-market economies (especially China, the Soviet Union, and Eastern Europe) in world trade, often expanding in disruptive directions because of grossly inefficient pricing and production decisions. Based heavily on barter, countertrade, and multitiered exchange rates, their trading activities generally must be considered as government-administered transactions. Barter, countertrade, and other forms of state trading are also expanding rapidly in a number of developing countries in the mid-1980s.

Thus, the emerging pattern of trade relations that can now be foreseen for the next several years is one of managed trade: a growing array of bilateral government-to-government arrangements, some special multilateral sectoral understandings among governments, heavy emphasis on shielding and assisting key domestic sectors, and growing direct participation of governments in trading activities. Because of these trends, trade officials increasingly are becoming caught up in the detailed administration of the volume and pricing of goods and services.

Although this trend may seem expedient for individual governments, it inevitably will have the cumulative effect of depressing world trade and retarding world economic growth.

Looking at the world marketplace in the second half of the 1980s, it can be easily conjectured that present trends will generate even greater turbulence and intergovernmental conflict than what was experienced in the 1970 to 1984 period.

The continuing debt plight of many developing countries must act as a spur to intensified global competition in many sectors—not only in labor-intensive products, but also up the value-added ladder in more technologically advanced products and services. When U.S. industrialists looked over their shoulders in the 1960s and early 1970s, they saw Japanese businesses running close behind. Now they see many "new Japans" or newly industrializing countries (NICs) following close behind both U.S. and Japanese enterprises.

In response to import pressures, key U.S. industries have called for, and received, increased restrictions on trade. The pattern of U.S. import protection measures in recent years has been characterized by two significant, but somewhat contradictory responses: greater reliance on "voluntary" export restraint understandings of an extra-legal character; and growing reliance on legally defined countermeasures to "unfair competition." Typical countermeasures in the latter category are antidumping and countervailing duty actions. Increasing resort to these types of actions represent a trend toward legalistic, highly technical forms of administrative harassment. What is "unfair" and what is "fair" is highly subjective. Some lawyers argue that the assessment of the degree of unfairness is based on clear principles. On the other hand, many economists and accountants claim that a high degree of judgment and arbitrariness enters the picture, because cost and price calculations within large, diversified, international enterprises are inevitably arbitrary.

However one evaluates these specific trends, the end results are growing barriers and distortions to trade, and growing uncertainty about potential new restrictions and distortions.

The predictability that should flow from adherence to international trading rules, particularly those embodied in GATT, is being overcome by uncertainties generated by actions and counteractions of national governments. Governments are trying to act autonomously and unilaterally, each seeking advantage over the others.

It would seem logical that, in such a deteriorating situation, governments might try to act together to restrain these diverse, mercantilist forces. But international economic cooperation among governments in the 1980s has been at its lowest ebb in the period since World War II. Multilateral cooperation is not really in vogue.

Calls for Multilateral Action

In the mid-1980s there has been a growing number of supporters of some kind of new multilateral effort to bring the present disruptive forces under control, restore confidence in liberal world markets, and repair the breakdown in international cooperation among governments. Prime Minister Nakasone of Japan, President Reagan, and a few other national leaders have called for moves in this direction. Many nations are reluctant, however, to start another round of liberalization or even to agree to narrow their own freedom of action.

Experience of the last three decades has shown that major multilateral negotiations, especially where they affect industry and agriculture directly, take a long time. The Kennedy Round took about seven years; the Multilateral Trade Negotiations, which ended in 1979, were actually conceived in 1967, and given formal impetus by ministers in 1973.

Even with the best intent, governments take time to restore international discipline and order in commercial relations through multilateral action. Major results cannot be anticipated in GATT, or in some cooperative GATT-IMF framework, for several years. There first must be a process of consensus-building internationally on both the institutional and substantive issues: How should GATT be strengthened? Should the United States rely more heavily on GATT procedures or continue the recent U.S. tendency toward reliance on unilateral action and bilateral problem-solving? Should GATT be more closely linked to other institutions, such as the IMF? What are the priority areas for new negotiations, and what principles should apply?

The inconclusive deliberations of the GATT ministerial meeting of November 1982 showed that there was little or no international consensus on such questions. Some governments have suggested that the disarray partly is due to U.S. uncertainty over objectives and procedures. Experience of the last three decades has shown that the premature raising of issues internationally, before the United States has clear ideas of its own, tends to result in international confusion and resistance to change on the part of many other governments.

What are the principal issues to be dealt with?

Agriculture and Basic Industries

The scope and magnitude of official intervention is greatest in agriculture and basic industries.

Fundamental problems arise in agriculture as a result of heavy intervention by every government in both production and trade, including heavy intervention by the U.S. government. Problems also arise because of erratic crop conditions, with varying periods of surplus and shortage that can give rise to wide swings in prices and severe cases of market disruption. Is it realistic to seek freer trade as such, or is it necessary for governments to manage markets, at least to the extent that policy conflicts among governments are constrained? Should governments try to assure adequate supplies of food in times of regional or global shortage, through multilaterial coordination of agricultural policies and cooperation in management of food reserves or buffer stocks?

In industry, the elaborate structure of negotiated protection in fiber, textiles, and apparel developed over 24 years still shows no sign of coming to an end, although its original intention was protection of a temporary character, with the objective of gradual liberalization. Instead, import protection in some countries, most notably the European Economic Community (EEC), has been made more strict. In steel, various mechanisms have been established to regulate volume and price of imports into the United States and the EEC, and there appears to be cartel-like cooperation in selling to other parts of the world, at least between Japanese and EEC producers. In petrochemicals, a "depression cartel" has evolved in Japan; producers in Western Europe are making arrangements to drop product lines, swap plants, and reduce capacity; and U.S. producers believe international "management" of trade and restructuring of this industry will soon be needed. The entry of additional suppliers benefitting from cheap feedstock, such as Saudi Arabia and Kuwait, will intensify these problems in the second half of the 1980s. Nonferrous metals producers feel threatened by increased capacity in developing countries and technological challenges from man-made substitutes, and some governments expect increased official aid and international cartelization in these sectors also will become necessary.

The growing challenge of Japan in world competition in high technology products and advanced production technologies has generated new fears in many industrial sectors in the United States and Europe. An array of formal and informal export restrictions has been put in place by the Japanese government in response to North American and European government requests and threats.

These are but examples. If trade is to be increasingly "managed," then are there better means than the present ad hoc responses to political pressures? If national industrial policies with trade implications are to be permitted, then how shall they be coordinated internationally to avoid international conflicts and distortions of trade and investment? What multilateral disciplines are needed to control the implementation of import "safeguard" actions that are designed to ease the economic and political pains of adjustment within nations?

Industrial Development and Technology Policies

In varying degrees, most governments have active policies to assist troubled industries and to encourage development of new industries. Subsidies, tax incentives, and other official aids are only part of such policies. "Buy national" policies are widespread in every country and are growing in scope everywhere. Investment performance requirements are used in one way or another by a majority of governments to promote domestic industries and job creation and to expand exports and encourage import substitution. Although such policies are to be found in most developing countries, they also characterize policies in key industrial sectors in Canada, France, Italy, and even the United Kingdom. Such policies are also prevalent in virtually all of world trade and in the production of military-related hardware and systems.

So-called "targeting" policies, which are said to characterize Japan, France, and some developing nations, may have some effect on the patterns of international competition in higher technology competition. The term "targeting" refers to policies that are aimed at nurturing and guiding development of key sectors while protecting them from international competition.

On the other hand, government-supported research and development (R&D) in West Germany, France, the United Kingdom, and the United States exceeds, as a share of the GNP, the level of official effort in countries like Japan (even for nondefense R&D by itself) where targeting is said to be more prominent. Much research in defense and space applications in the United States and Western Europe is having more direct and more immediate commercial significance than might have been true a decade ago (for example, fiber optics, ceramics and composites, high speed integrated circuits, and sensors). Much more of U.S. government-supported R&D results in "dual use" processes and products today than was true in the early 1960s.

Some private enterprises have moved toward full-scale cross-border cooperation in development of new technologies as well as in production and sale of products (for example, in robotics and other aspects of industrial automation). Is this an alternative answer, and if so, what does it mean for antitrust and other competition policies on the national and the international levels?

Can industrial technology policies be brought into concert on the international level, and if so, under what kind of rules or discipline? Can governments improve the environment for global technological advances while maintaining the value of proprietary rights and ensuring liberal market conditions? Can government efforts to control out-

6

flow of technology be made more consistent with private efforts to assure inflow of technology—that is, access to technologies developed in other countries? What should be the rules of the road for equitable two-way traffic, including foreign participation in government-supported research? Can or should government assistance to R&D be put under multilateral constraints, or should governments be left free to assist development of new technologies as they see fit? What are appropriate private enterprise responses to government-assisted competition in other nations?

Trade in Services

Much public recognition has been given in the United States to the growing importance of services in world commerce. Industries and governments alike thus far have failed, however, to articulate the general character of presently perceived problems and have failed to lay out a coherent strategy or conceptual framework for negotiations. This has given rise to deep suspicions in many countries that the United States has no other purpose than to dominate the world services business by preventing any form of intervention by other nations.

The generic problems must be analyzed and basic principles be developed that can help form the basis of a new international consensus. Prominent in such a new framework would be the right to deliver services in all markets and relatively unimpeded use of global delivery systems, which in most cases will be computer-telecommunications networks.

Beyond these issues, what should be done about existing international service organizations? What about state monopolies? What should be the legitimate roles of governments in maintaining security of information flows, reliability of services, adequacy of communications channels, defense of national sovereignty and security, etc.?

East-West Trade

Until recently, the management of East-West commercial relations did not give rise to major international policy disputes and only rarely caused disruption to private business. National policies tended to be designed in response to particular problems or with reference to particular technologies. International coordination of strategic export controls worked with reasonable success, in spite of continuing irritations among Western governments. Treatment of nonmarket economies—Soviet bloc, People's Republic of China, etc.—was ad hoc, both

7

bilaterally and multilaterally. Special arrangements were made in GATT for accession of countries like Poland and Hungary, so as to differentiate them from other Council for Mutual Economic Assistance (COMECON) nations.

These ad hoc arrangements were satisfactory until recently. The role of Nonmarket Economies (NMEs) in the trade and industrial performance of Western Europe and Japan has grown significantly in recent years, however. Motivations and interests now vary more widely within the West, and national policies are rapidly diverging. The recent U.S.-European dispute over the Yamal gas pipeline from the Soviet Union to Western Europe dramatized underlying differences in both political and economic judgments among the Western nations.

In GATT, the gradual involvement of the People's Republic of China and recent exploratory moves by the Soviet Union threaten to disturb the ad hoc, relaxed approach taken in the past toward the NMEs in GATT.

The growing role of NME-generated barter, buy-back trade, and other countertrade in world markets also raises serious issues (for example, in fertilizers, petrochemicals, machinery, commodities).

Can GATT be restructured to provide special but separate rules and procedures for relations between market and nonmarket nations? Can better rules be devised on the international level to cope with increased trade of NMEs? Can the handling of security and technology issues be improved by changing the venue to other institutions or by changing the criteria for cooperation in management of trade, investment, and technology flows among the Western nations? What new challenges to East-West trade controls are posed by the rapid growth of on-line technology exchange among scientists and engineers worldwide through computer-telecommunications networks?

Barter and Other Nonmarket Transactions

In addition to East-West nonmarket trade, many other nations are expanding barter activity under pressure from their international debt service and credit limitations. The scope of such nonmarket activities is now estimated to be in the range of 20 to 30 percent of total world trade. What new rules need to be devised to cope with the potential disruptive effects of such business activities?

Finance and Trade

Export credit continues to be a source of conflict among the major trading nations, and some developing nations are beginning to emerge as serious competitors in the game of subsidized finance—Brazil for example. Recent efforts to bring about multilateral order and discipline have been relatively ineffective. Are there more arbitrary, but effective, rules that can be devised—for example, banning soft credits on any sales from one developed country to another? Are there better ways to set international guidelines, or is the only really effective tool a massive "war chest?" If the latter, what should be the ultimate objective of an all-out subsidy war?

How can the financial and trade policies of the major economies be brought into greater harmony and consistency? At present, trade and financial officials give opposite advice. GATT and the IMF have only a limited relationship. Moreover, the World Bank and other multilateral development banks often support development of industries in developing countries that are already characterized by excess capacity on the world market level.

National monetary policies are often devised without regard to trade consequences (and in the United States one could say there is almost a willful neglect by monetary officials of the trade consequences of their decisions). Can macroeconomic policy management be improved on both the national and international level to ensure that exchange rate effects and effects on financial flows are taken into account, and that gross distortions in exchange rates are corrected—the yen-dollar relationship for example?

North-South Relations

Can the present wave of economic pragmatism in developing countries, induced by the world financial crisis, be used to persuade developing countries to adopt more liberal, market-oriented trade policies as part of their reorientation programs? Is this the right historical moment to force North-South discussions and negotiations into a more economically sound multilateral framework of rights and obligations? How fast can "graduation" of key developing countries take place in the face of the massive debt crises they now face? What kind of agenda for negotiations can be devised that offers real benefits to developing countries in exchange for opening their own markets?

Global Nondiscrimination versus Differentiated Trading Relationships

The multilateral, nondiscriminatory Most Favored Nation (MFN) framework traditionally has been central to U.S. trade policies. A substantial part of world trade has been subsumed under special trade arrangements within Western Europe and between the EEC and many "associated" countries in the Mediterranean, Africa, Middle East and the Asian Pacific, however. Further enlargement of the EEC will tend to "lock up" potential as well as actual trade and investment flows.

Should the United States continue its global, nondiscriminatory orientation, or are there instances in which a differentiated policy may be desirable? For example, the problems that arise between the United States, on the one hand, and Mexico and Canada on the other, could be managed in bilateral "special relationships" that recognize the contiguity of territories and the intense interaction of these national economies. Conversely, if "special arrangements" are not made, what are the risks of serious economic and political confrontations?

Would further exploration by the United States of "special" bilateral arrangements cause a serious deterioration in the Most Favored Nation structure of GATT, and if so, what should be done to establish new rules that apply to relations between groups of countries covered by discriminatory arrangements?

The Role of Government and Law

In the United States, an adversary relationship continues to prevail between business and government in relation to world trade and investment, whereas business and government are viewed in many other countries as partners in a common endeavor. Can or should the public-private relationship be changed in the United States, and if so, in what ways? Are consultative committees enough?

The U.S. government traditionally has been organized around domestic political, social, and economic preoccupations, with external economic relations given lower priority. One consequence is that responsibility for trade policy and the administration of trade laws is shared among a wide range of agencies, interagency committees, and presidential staff. Can or should the U.S. government pull together in one agency all the strands of foreign economic policy, or of foreign trade and investment policy, or of industrial trade policy? Or should there be a more serious effort to coordinate policies without fundamentally altering the existing decision structure?

The Constitution provides that Congress, not the president, shall regulate foreign commerce. This creates certain special difficulties between the executive branch and Congress that are handled by elaborate legislation, delegating powers to the executive branch yet closely circumscribing their use. The trend in legislative drafting in recent years has been to limit more and more the administrative discretion of the executive branch in initiating actions when faced with private petitions for action. Indeed, the U.S. trade law has become so elaborate that some other governments consider the legalistic intricacy of the U.S. trade laws to be a monstrous nontariff barrier.

Should the laws continue to evolve in this technical direction, or should there be an effort to simplify? When private parties seek government action, particularly for import protection, what quid pro quo should be asked that would ensure that the national interest is taken adequately into account?

Conflicts between U.S. and foreign laws, particularly with respect to extraterritoriality, are increasingly frequent and disruptive to world business. What changes in U.S. law and administrative practice are needed to improve the climate for trade and investment and prevent arbitrary disruption to traditional economic activities? Should a multilateral code be sought that would place constraints on all manifestations of extraterritoriality by all governments?

Facing Tomorrow's Problems and Opportunities

We are entering a new period of industrial revolution, driven by technology and the global redeployment of industry. International competitiveness of sectors will depend on the adaptation of industries and services to the new world market realities.

Until now, when industrial difficulties have been perceived, government policies in the United States and Western Europe usually have aimed at shoring up troubled sectors. Keeping old enterprises in operation often is viewed as a means of preserving jobs. Such policies could well be described as "adjustment resistance" policies. Government officials tend to have little knowledge of new technologies, new products, and new markets. Decisions are based on past experiences— policy is devised by looking back at old problems rather than by looking forward to new opportunities. Is there some way in which government, industry, academics, and other scientists can exchange views and develop a "perspective" on the major thrusts of technology and their potential effects? Can this be done without risking increased intervention by the government in efforts to "plan" the U.S. economy?

In what ways can domestic policies be improved to facilitate structural adjustment rather than impede it? Can policies be devised that would strengthen the technological thrusts of the U.S. economy? For example, could the U.S. government improve the management of its own R&D programs in agriculture, space, and defense so as to bring

11

about faster diffusion to the private sector of government-sponsored research? Should greater intercompany cooperation be allowed within the United States in development of new technologies— as is common in Japan, West Germany, or France for example? What else can be done to encourage R&D and the commercial application of new technologies?

Fears are expressed that we are in danger of losing critical industries that are part of the vital foundation of our economy. Is this really true, or are we approaching a time when new products will replace old, and new basic industries will take over the traditional roles of the steel and other metal producers, etc.?

Most important of all, competitiveness in the future will depend on human resources. Industrial jobs will continue to decline as a share of total employment because of automation. Services will continue to expand. This raises profound questions about education and retraining. Lifetime education and "retooling" of people may become essential if a high level of unemployment is to be avoided.

Thus, sound trade policies will require sound domestic economic policies—policies that recognize the reality that the United States is part of a global marketplace characterized by rapid change. We can no longer act as if the U.S. economy is separate from the international flows of capital, technology, trade, and services. Domestic fiscal and monetary policy have to be geared to international as well as domestic realities. The results of a strong dollar do matter in accelerating the long-term shift to services and in intensifying structural adjustment difficulties of traditional manufacturing industries.

Finally, sound trade policy must be focused on future potential rather than on business complaints about past problems. We have losers; but we also have winners. To maintain world economic leadership, we must run faster; but we cannot run well by looking backwards.

Moreover, because international trade negotiations are inevitably slow, taking several years, it is imperative that negotiating objectives be devised in relation to future contingencies rather than to past problems. Because future problems cannot be readily foreseen, stress must be placed on fundamental principles of how governments should react to, and handle, trade disputes and domestic structural adjustment difficulties. Most governments will not take seriously any effort aimed at negotiating new international principles, however, unless the major trading nations show a willingness to work within the framework of multilateral rules. In the 1970s and 1980s, the major trading nations frequently have tried to avoid the constraints imposed by multilateral rules and instead have acted outside the rules in an extralegal manner.

12

There is not much point in negotiating new world trade rules unless the governments concerned expect to subordinate their own national policies to the new rules. Ultimately, this poses the critical question in trade policy: Will governments yield some of their present freedom of action in exchange for a more predictable, stable, liberal trade environment?

Outlook for U.S. Economic Diplomacy: Europe and the Pacific Basin

by
John N. Yochelson

U.S. resurgence has been the dominant factor in the world economy of the mid-1980s. The U.S. rebound of 1983-1984, in the wake of a severe slump, produced some spectacular figures: real gross national product (GNP) growth averaged almost 5.5 percent, including one spurt in double digits; inflation held below 3.5 percent; unemployment dropped from 10.8 percent to 7.4 percent; productivity rose at levels unseen since the 1960s; capital investment boomed.[1] Although the explosive rate of growth has slowed lately, the United States is enjoying at least a robust cyclical recovery if not a much more lasting improvement in economic performance.

To be sure, there have been troubling sides to U.S. resurgence. The U.S. merchandise trade deficit reached $123 billion in 1984 and is projected to widen.[2] Federal deficits may exceed $200 billion in the coming fiscal year according to the Office of Management and Budget. Interest rates, although dropping sharply from 1980 levels, have remained stubbornly high.

Moreover, the forces in play in the U.S. economy continue to confound many experts. Trade deficits should weaken the dollar, yet the dollar has soared. Government borrowing should crowd out private investment, yet private investment has climbed. Interest rates should decline in the face of low inflation, yet they persist. The result has been not just a nightmare for economic forecasting but a contentious debate over the sustainability and global impact of the U.S. recovery.

Pessimists versus Optimists

Pessimists both in the United States and abroad hold that the underpinnings of the U.S. recovery are weak and that its costs to the world economy substantial. In their view, the U.S. economic engine has been fueled by massive federal budget deficits. The high rates of return needed to finance the deficits have attracted huge flows of scarce foreign capital. These, in turn, have driven the dollar to levels far

15

beyond those warranted by comparisons of purchasing power of the U.S. economy. Pessimists claim that the overvalued dollar has undercut the competitive position of U.S. industry, costing hundreds of thousands of jobs in both export and import-competing sectors. The run up of the dollar also has added greatly to the burden on foreigners of servicing their international debt, most of which is denominated in U.S. currency and keyed to the U.S. prime rate. Further, it has constrained the policies of Europe and Japan, forcing up their interest rates to check capital outflow.[3]

Pessimists see a bleak future unless drastic steps are taken to reduce U.S. interest and exchange rates by cutting the federal government's borrowing requirements. If far-reaching measures—including tax increases—are not taken at once, the richest nation in the world will move rapidly into a net debtor position, the tide of protectionism will become overwhelming, confidence in the U.S. economy will ebb, and a precipitous, destabilizing fall of the dollar will inevitably occur.

Optimists paint a very different picture. For them, the United States has been the vital locomotive pulling the rest of the world out of recession. U.S. growth and U.S. imports have pumped timely demand into the global economy. An open U.S. market has helped U.S. trading partners, both in the developed and the developing world, far more than the strong dollar has hurt them. Optimists see the U.S. resurgence as solidly grounded. It is, above all, the new dynamism of the U.S. business environment that is drawing in capital from abroad. Whereas pessimists see imports deindustrializing the United States, optimists see a hold on inflation and a spur to increased productivity. The strong dollar has caused some dislocation and hardship, but the loss of jobs in older industries has been more than compensated by the creation of new job opportunities.[4]

Optimists concede that the U.S. trade and budget deficits cannot be sustained over the long term. They do not, however, share the sense of dire urgency of pessimists. They see global recovery and continued domestic growth helping to redress current imbalances. They contend that there is enough time to take needed corrective measures. Looking ahead, optimists anticipate a gradual reduction of the deficits, a "soft" landing for the dollar, and a superior competitive position for U.S. industry as global economic recovery proceeds.

The contrasting views of optimists and pessimists highlight differing implications of the U.S. upturn on the world economy.

For pessimists, U.S. policy remains the central factor in the global economic equation. It is up to Washington to assure a balanced worldwide recovery. The projection of current policies will not allow for

16

such a recovery. They are bound to drive the United States inward economically and, in the long term, politically.

For optimists, the United States has already generated powerful momentum for global economic expansion and much of the needed initiative now lies with U.S. trading partners. Since mid-1982 the United States has absorbed more than 65 percent of non-Organization of Petroleum Exporting Countries (non-OPEC) developing country exports and almost 85 percent of the increase in Latin American exports.[5] At the same time, the surge in U.S. demand has provided a tremendous boost to the Organization for Economic Cooperation and Development (OECD) economies. Sustained global recovery now depends in large measure on Europe's capacity to revitalize itself, Japan's ability to address the problems created by its enormous trade surplus, and the newly industrializing countries' willingness to integrate themselves more fully into the trading system. The United States can exert leadership in managing the world economy by example and through negotiation without any radical shift in current policy.

The landslide reelection of Ronald Reagan confirmed that optimists will set U.S. policy for the next several years—at least in the executive branch.

In the meantime, three enduring effects of U.S. resurgence are already discernible. First, U.S. achievements have spurred intensive self-assessment in Europe. The demonstration that there is an alternative to low growth and high inflation has been acknowledged by Europeans of all political colors and led many to adjust their thinking in the light of recent U.S. achievements.

Second, while Europe has been looking toward the United States, the United States has been looking toward the Pacific rim. The deterioration of the U.S. trade position, the U.S. preoccupation with competitiveness, and the dynamism of the Pacific rim nations have all converged to bring this region— not Europe—to the forefront of U.S. concern over future challenges and opportunities.

Third, U.S. economic diplomacy has grown increasingly assertive. The Reagan administration has pressed hard for an approach to the international economic agenda that gives greater play to market forces and the role of the private sector. Washington also has reacted forcefully in bilateral and multilateral negotiations to a massive and growing trade deficit. The outlook is for further U.S. assertiveness.

Together, these developments signal an important new phase in U.S. relations with key trading partners.

Europe and the U.S. Example

Recent U.S. achievements have very much captured the attention of Europe. European criticism of U.S. budget deficits and interest rates has by no means ended, but the force of the U.S. recovery and the advantages it has generated are now widely conceded. During the past year, "Reagan's miracle" has been widely covered in the media, extensively analyzed, and acknowleged by politicians of the left and right.

Although the recent strength of the U.S. economy has clearly impressed Europeans, the cyclical recovery per se has not been the primary focus of their interest. Rather, the vigor of the recovery has raised the question of whether the United States is coping more effectively than Europe with longer-term challenges of structural change and adjustment.

Since the early 1970s, all of the advanced industrial economies have been swept by forces of deep, and in some instances, disruptive change:

- ◆ The energy price shocks of 1973-1974 and 1979 wrenched cost and price structures worldwide. The fivefold real increase in petroleum prices fueled inflation, triggered a major flow of financial resources to oil- producing nations, and forced far-reaching adjustment in the energy-intensive industrial bases of the West.

- ◆ The maturing of the less developed countries emerged as a fundamental factor in the world economy during the 1970s. The newly industrializing countries, in particular, became increasingly significant markets for Western exports but also pressed their comparative advantage in old-line, technologically simpler, labor intensive industries. Global capacity in these industries has increased far more rapidly than demand, yet pressures on the developing countries to increase market share have only intensified.

- ◆ The pace of technological innovation has accelerated dramatically, promising gains in growth and productivity but also transforming skill requirements for the labor force, manufacturing processes, and the provision of services. The diffusion of technology has both generated opportunities and brought dislocation at unprecedented speed.

- ◆ Demand for public sector services has risen relentlessly. The public sector share of GNP has increased in all of the advanced economies, driven in large part by escalating outlays for health, education, and welfare.[6]

18

At the most general level, these changes had similar effects on both sides of the Atlantic. Investment, productivity, and growth slowed in both the United States and OECD Europe in the 1970s. Consistent macroeconomic policies could not be sustained in the face of inflationary pressures. Dislocations of the work force occurred in many of the same "sunset" industries: textiles and apparel, leather goods, iron and steel, ship building, and nonferrous metals. Rates of unemployment increased, and the number of jobless who could not be absorbed into the labor market even in high periods of activity (the structurally unemployed) ratcheted upward in successive business cycles.

The Reagan administration took office in 1981 with definite views regarding the policies needed to cope with these challenges. Its premise was that economic growth was the most constructive motor for change and adaptation. The central policy objectives of the administration were to wring inflation out of the economy, reduce the size and influence of government, and to improve the business climate. The linchpin of the Reagan program was the Economic Recovery Act of 1981, which mandated a three-year, 25 percent tax cut and provided significant new incentives for business investment. This legislation was supplemented by a strong push for government deregulation, which had begun under the Carter administration, and a determined effort to pare entitlements spending.

It is unrealistic to attribute the strong overall performance of the U.S. economy just to the policies of one administration. The decline in world oil prices, the size and integration of the world capital market, and the flexibility of U.S. labor and management have all been powerful assets. By the same token, however, there is no doubt that the policy thrust of the Reagan administration and the effective exercise of presidential leadership have made an enormous difference. The impetus given to private sector growth has altered the political, economic, and psychological setting in the United States. In this way, the White House has minimized the impact of the actual increase in the public sector share of GNP that has taken place.

The net impact of the Reagan program has been to force the pace of change in the U.S. economy. On the one hand, the recession and the strong dollar have compelled firms to streamline operations and increase productivity. On the other, fiscal incentives, deregulation, and large inflows of foreign capital have powered an extraordinary expansion.

The resulting crucible has accelerated several widely known long-term trends in the U.S. economy: (1) the growth of the work force; (2) the shift of resources from the goods-producing to the services sector;

(3) the shift within manufacturing toward technology-intensive industries.[7] The job-creating capacity of the economy was impressively demonstrated during the 1970s when the entry of the baby boom generation and the addition of women of all ages increased the size of the work force by 20 million. Nearly 6 million more jobs were added during the first Reagan administration, although demographic pressures began to recede.[8] The bulk of new jobs are being generated in the services sector, which has not only grown faster than the goods-producing sector but proved more resilient through cyclical downturns. Whereas employment in manufacturing had not recovered to prerecession levels by the end of 1983, 1.5 million new employees were added to services' payrolls during that year alone.[9] The decline in manufacturing employment has been concentrated in import-competing, basic industries using standardized technologies—primary metals, shoes, textiles, apparel, and automobiles. Strong gains in output, productivity, and employment have been registered in high-technology industries. A transformation of the manufacturing sector has only been speeded as basic industries have turned increasingly to advanced technology in order to compete.

The tempo of change and adjustment in the United States strikes a vivid contrast with Europe. First, OECD Europe has dramatically underperformed the United States in job creation. The size of the European work force has remained flat since the early 1970s, in sharp opposition to the U.S. record. The inability to generate new jobs has converted a once tight labor market into one of oversupply, leaving severe problems of youth and extended-duration unemployment. The lag in investment, the increase of real wages at a faster rate than productivity, the rigidity of labor markets, and the rise in benefits for the unemployed have all contributed to a pattern of sustained stagnation.[10]

Second, the shift into services has taken place more slowly in Europe than in the United States. The public sector rather than the private sector, moreover, has accounted for the lion's share of new employment in services.

Third, Europe has had great difficulty in reshaping its basic industries. Resistance to change has been particularly strong in coal mining, steel, and metal working. At the same time, Europe's high-technology base has not developed as rapidly as that of the United States or Japan.

There certainly is no easy U.S. cure for Europe's persistent problems of growth and structural adjustment. European economies themselves vary so widely in size, structure, performance, and policy outlook—

and the differences between any of them and the United States are so wide—that one can at best suggest a U.S. example.

Recent U.S. experience points away from a number of policy directions that have been advanced in the swirling debate over Europe's economic future: job sharing; increased use of industrial policies; moves to restrict the mobility of labor and capital (i.e., the Vredling proposal).

Instead, the U.S. example points Europe toward

- giving greater priority to the acceleration rather than the cushioning of change;
- reducing the size and scope of public sector involvement in national economies;
- improving the entrepreneurial climate.

European movement along these policy lines looks encouraging. The objectives of increasing factor mobility, cutting structural budget deficits, and tapping the energies of the private sector have all moved up on the agendas of European governments across the board.[11] The convergence of European and U.S. perspectives, however, has hardly stilled criticism of U.S. macroeconomic policy as a major constraint on Europe's still modest cyclical recovery.[12]

On balance, Europe remains ambivalent about U.S. economic resurgence—stunned by the results yet still skeptical of some of the policies that brought them about.

The Pull of the Pacific Rim

While European interest in the strengths of the U.S. economy has heightened, the Pacific rim has increasingly caught both the attention and the imagination of the United States. The deepening of U.S. economic involvement in East Asia has not been recent. Two-way trade across the Pacific surpassed trans-Atlantic trade in 1980.[13] During the past several years, however, this shift has been confirmed as a longer-term trend. The Pacific Basin is now hailed almost routinely by the media as well as business and government as the hub of the future world economy. No comparable Atlantic vision is focusing debate.

The economic profile of the Pacific Basin has eclipsed that of Europe because the Pacific rim is widely regarded by Americans as both a region of greater opportunity and a more severe competitive threat.

The opportunities of the Pacific Basin—with its vast market potential and abundant natural resources—need little elaboration. The growth of the Pacific rim nations has outstripped the rest of the world since

21

the first oil shock: Japan has been a relative laggard in the region averaging about 5 percent real growth; the ASEAN nations as a whole have achieved 7 percent growth, while growth rates in Korea, Taiwan, and Hong Kong have surpassed all others.[14] In addition, the opening of the People's Republic of China to the West offers the historic possibility of integrating the world's largest market into the global economy. The Reagan administration has made a major effort to call attention to the political and economic potential of the Pacific Basin.[15]

Clearly, East Asia poses economic challenges of a different order from Europe. Whereas nearly 50 percent of total U.S. direct investment overseas is in Europe, the Pacific rim counts for less than 15 percent (although the rate of growth of U.S. investment in East Asia has nearly doubled that of investment in Europe since the mid-1970s).[16] U.S. multinationals have operated effectively within the European Community since its creation but must bridge more significant cultural differences in the Pacific Basin. Although Europe has provided vital export markets for U.S. agriculture, technology, and services, it is still not regarded by many Americans as a decisive competitive threat. 1984 marked the first year since 1972 that the European Community ran a trade surplus with the United States.

The dynamism of the East Asian nations, on the other hand, has raised profound questions regarding the U.S. competitive position. Japan, Korea, Taiwan, Hong Kong, and Singapore accounted for roughly one-half of the $130 billion U.S. merchandise trade deficit in 1984.[17] The composition of U.S. trade with East Asia—in contrast to U.S.-European trade—has been highly asymmetrical: virtually all U.S. imports are in manufactures while U.S. exports are weighted heavily toward raw materials, agricultural goods and services. Korea, Taiwan, Singapore, and Hong Kong have pressed the United States on the low end of the industrial mix and are moving rapidly upscale. At the least, Japan has reached parity in most of the advanced technologies. It is the Pacific Basin that has sparked a searching U.S. domestic debate over competitiveness and evoked a determined response from U.S. industry.

The U.S. concentration on the Pacific rim, both as partner and rival, does not force a choice for U.S. policy between Europe and East Asia. Fears that a U.S. tilt toward the Pacific rim could downgrade Atlantic priorities underrate both the importance of U.S. economic stakes in Europe and the crucial significance of the U.S.-Soviet rivalry. By the same token, fears of a protectionist U.S. backlash against East Asia discount both U.S. geopolitical stakes in the Pacific and the open market predilections of the Reagan administration. Nevertheless, U.S.

resurgence has confirmed the end of an era in which the United States and Europe were the dominant forces shaping the global economic order. If current trends continue, U.S. policies and perspectives on the world economy will be increasingly influenced by a U.S.-East Asian dynamic over which Europe has diminshed control.

U.S. Assertiveness

Another development with which all U.S. trading partners will have to reckon is the renewed assertiveness of U.S. economic diplomacy. To be sure, the United States has played a commanding role in the international economy since the establishment of the Bretton Woods system. During the last several years, however, the Reagan administration has pressed its views with a firmness not seen since the closing of the gold window and the devaluation of the dollar in 1971.

Three sources of renewed U.S. assertiveness stand out. First, the administration brought with it a vision of the world economy that it was determined to make operational.[18] This vision saw sound, domestic policies of the world's key economies as the foundation of a prosperous world economy. It emphasized the need for convergence of national economic policies around the fundamentals of low inflation and greater reliance on market forces both internally and internationally. Approaches to the international economic agenda were to arise out of discrete national decisions rather than a global blueprint. The administration has applied these principles rigorously at the annual economic summits of major Western leaders, in deliberations over the funding and policies of the International Monetary Fund (IMF) and the World Bank, and in other international forums.

Second, in the East-West context, the Reagan administration has insisted more strenuously than its predecessors that Western commercial interests be subordinated to strategic considerations. The use of U.S. leverage to contain leakage of high technology to the Soviet bloc has reflected an effort to redefine the framework of East-West relations that developed during the 1970s.

Third, bulging deficits have toughened the U.S. trade stance. The appreciation of the dollar has spurred a major push—directed mainly at Japan and a number of developing countries—to improve U.S. market access overseas. At the same time, the surge of imports that has accompanied the cyclical recovery of the U.S. economy has intensified protectionist pressures. The Reagan administration has contained the most severe of these pressures, but it has also restricted access to the U.S. market through the selective use of tariffs, quotas, and voluntary export restraint agreements covering automobiles, textiles, footwear, steel, and consumer electronics. Trade legislation passed in October 1984 simplified procedures for seeking import relief and it introduced U.S. access to foreign markets in services, high technology, and investment as a potential consideration for gaining entry into the U.S. market. In addition, the administration has cracked down on counterfeiting and tightened the administering of customs regulations.

At the same time, the United States has adopted a more hard-nosed approach than some of its trading partners expected to a prospective new round of General Agreement on Tariffs and Trade (GATT) negotiations. Instead of concentrating all its effort on a push for across-the-board GATT talks involving more than 100 countries, the administration has offered to negotiate selectively on a range of specific trade issues with any nation ready to begin bilateral negotiations. In so doing, the United States by no means ruled out an early multilateral GATT round but served notice that it is prepared to explore fresh avenues to the trade agenda.

Continued U.S. assertiveness lies ahead. The Reagan administration will press its major trading partners on the same fundamentals that have energized the U.S. economy and improved global prospects. The Pacific Basin challenge will not recede. Looming trade deficits will move the United States to pursue its trade interests more strongly than ever, but not at the expense of the administration's underlying commitment to open world markets.

Notes

1. *OECD Economic Outlook*, no. 36, December 1984.

2. "Strong Dollar Blamed for Trade Deficit," *Washington Post*, January 20, 1984.

3. See, for example, C. Fred Bergsten, "Currency Crisis," *New York Times*, September 23, 1983.

4. See, for example, "A Forward Look at Foreign Policy," speech by Secretary of State George Shultz, October 19, 1984; "World Economic Prospects," speech by Under Secretary of State for Economic Affairs Allen Wallis, July 27, 1984.

5. Speech by Assistant Secretary of State for Economic and Business Affairs Richard McCormack, November 22, 1984.

6. See *OECD Economic Outlook*, no. 36.

7. For a review of these trends, see *Annual Report of the President of the United States on the Trade Agreements Program*, 27th issue, 1983.

8. *Wall Street Journal*, November 5, 1984.

9. *Annual Report of the President of the United States on the Trade Agreements Program.*

10. For an assessment of this trend, see the collection of essays in *Unemployment and Growth in the Western Economies*, Andrew J. Pierce, ed. (New York, N.Y.: Council on Foreign Relations, 1984).

11. Jean-François Revel and Branko Lavitch, "Continental Mainstream is a Free-Market Current," *Wall Street Journal*, December 12, 1984.

12. See, for example, Shirley Williams, "Unemployment and Economic Strains in the Western Alliance," in *Unemployment and Growth in the Western Economies*.

13. "Asia Replaces Europe as Major Partner," *Washington Post*, April 22, 1984.

14. "Far East Sprints Economically but Crawls Politically," *Wall Street Journal*, July 23, 1984.

15. See, for example, "Europe v. Asia: Is Diplomacy a Zero-Sum Game?" speech by Deputy Secretary of State Kenneth Dam, August 6, 1984; "Challenges Facing the U.S. and ASEAN," speech by Secretary of State George Shultz, July 13, 1984; "The U.S. and East Asia: A Partnership for the Future," speech by Secretary of State George Shultz, March 3, 1983.

16. *International Direct Investment: Global Trends and the U.S. Role*, U.S. Department of Commerce, August 1984.

17. "Gains Seen in Global Economy," *Washington Post*, January 20, 1984.

18. For a perceptive analysis of the Reagan administration view, see Henry R. Nau, *International Reaganomics: A Domestic Approach to World Economy* (Washington, D.C.: Center for Strategic and International Studies, 1984).

The Linkage between International Trade and Financial Policy

by
Jonathan D. Aronson and Paul R. Krugman

Despite the strong U.S. economic recovery in 1983 and 1984, the stability of both the world financial system and the trading system remain in doubt. Their vulnerabilities are closely linked. The rising protectionist pressures that threaten world trade have some of their roots in a malfunctioning of the international financial system; yet trade must expand to safeguard the financial system and ensure long-term global economic growth. More than ever, the leadership to take us through the next decade must involve integrating trade and financial policy.

The U.S. policy-making apparatus is not organized for this sort of integration. Here, and in most other advanced countries, issues of international economic policy are sorted into two separate boxes. On one side is international trade policy—tariffs, quotas, dumping. On the other side is international financial policy —exchange rates, balance of payments adjustment, regulation of international capital flows. Trade policy is the responsibility of trade ministers—in the United States, the U.S. trade representative and the secretary of commerce. Financial policy is the responsibility of finance ministers and central bankers—here, the secretary of the treasury and the chairman of the Federal Reserve Board. This division of responsibility is reproduced in the structure of international organizations; where the General Agreement on Tariffs and Trade (GATT) has primary responsibility for trade, and the International Monetary Fund (IMF) has primary responsibility for finance.

The distinction between trade and financial issues was always artificial, but until the late 1960s it worked fairly well. As long as the world economy experienced steady growth, with increasing liberalization of trade and mostly stable exchange rates, ad hoc coordination of trade and financial policy usually sufficed. But the conditions changed, and what worked before is not enough now. We live in a much more turbulent, interdependent world economy than we used to, one in which trade and financial issues interact in powerful ways.

27

Although the initial crisis has eased somewhat, global debt problems still could undermine both the efficient operation of the international financial framework and world trade. Since the debt crisis struck in August 1982, less developed countries (LDC) imports slowed as debtors struggled to conserve funds needed to meet their debt obligations. At the same time, debtors worked to maintain or increase their exports to generate foreign exchange. Latin American trade surpluses of 1983 and early 1984 helped these countries avoid financial disaster, but the tensions created by these opposing policies cannot be ignored indefinitely. Trade—both imports and exports—will have to be an important contributor to any long-term solution to the debt situation.

Although LDC debt problems provoked most of the recent attention to trade-finance linkages, interactions among the industrialized countries cannot be ignored. Exchange rate movements are now a major factor in shifting trade competitiveness, both in shaping the formation of trade policy and themselves being affected by the market's expectations of future trade policy.

The growing importance of the links between trade and financial policy simultaneously creates new dangers and new opportunities. The danger is that if trade and financial policy continue to be made in relative isolation, their unplanned, unanticipated interaction could lead to a kind of "vicious circle," in which a deteriorating international financial environment leads countries into trade policies that further weaken the financial system and slow or abort global economic recovery. The opportunity rests on the possibility that if we can devise mutually reinforcing trade and financial policies, they may be more effective than the sum of their parts, creating a "virtuous circle" of mutually reinforcing success.

This paper sketches out some of the linkages between trade and financial policy, the risks created by these linkages, and policy options for minimizing the risks.

International Debt and Trade

The Setting

The 1970s were a golden era for North-South lending. The availability of funds from the Organization of Petroleum Exporting Countries (OPEC) surplus led banks to look overseas for markets, and the banks were drawn to the most advanced developing countries. These countries began to borrow heavily to finance their development; yet for much of the 1970s there seemed little reason for concern about their growing debt. The exports of borrowing countries grew rapidly in volume. More important, in the inflationary environment of the 1970s the dollar value of their exports rose far faster. Interest rates, though high by earlier standards, failed to keep up with inflation. Everything seemed to suggest that the old rules concerning what constituted responsible limits on borrowing and lending no longer applied.

Whether the banks overlent or the countries overborrowed is irrelevant. The important point is that after the second oil shock in 1979, the ground shifted and the ability of some large borrowers to service their debts deteriorated. The most serious international recession in decades produced a stagnation in both the volumes and the prices of LDC exports. At the same time, interest rates rose to unprecedented heights.

The result was a crisis of lender confidence, beginning with Mexico in August 1982. By the end of 1982, Brazil, Argentina, Mexico, and several smaller countries were forced into rescheduling debt and adopting emergency programs of domestic austerity. These programs in turn caused a substantial drop in U.S. exports to most of the key debtor nations that translated into lost U.S.jobs.

The current situation is one of forced austerity by debtor countries and forced lending, along with significant loan rescheduling, by their bankers, with the IMF effectively dictating the behavior of both sets of players. The debtor countries cannot fully service their existing debt; but the IMF demands that they make extreme sacrifices to service as much as possible. At the same time, the IMF leans on the bankers to continue to lend new funds and to reschedule existing debts to the extent necessary. In effect, under pressure from the IMF, banks have relent a part of the interest coming due or stretched out the repayment periods of loans. In September 1984, for example, banks postponed payment of $48.5 billion of Mexico's debt principal as a "reward" for its austerity program.

In this setting each set of players is hostage to the other:

- ◆ The banks cannot recoup their loans if the countries refuse to pay, and the countries cannot do business with the world if the banks call them in default;
- ◆ The small banks would like to pull out and have others inject funds in their place, but they cannot rely on others and will suffer along with every other creditor if an overall crisis is provoked;
- ◆ The large banks and the official creditors also would like to reduce their exposure but cannot trust that others will make up the lost funds;

♦ The borrowers threaten that without more money or decreased debt servicing requirements they will be unable to meet their current obligations, although creditors threaten to cut off further funds unless borrowers undertake extreme domestic adjustment.

The IMF stands in the middle, pressuring debtor countries to impose harsh austerity measures that the debtors would not accept politically if mandated by creditor countries or the banks. At the same time, the IMF spurs the banks toward greater leniency toward the borrowers.

Risks of a Downward Spiral

To date, the IMF, the banks, and both debtor and creditor country governments have nimbly worked out last minute financial compromises and made necessary domestic adjustments. The debtors have accepted more austerity for a longer period than at first seemed probable. The banks swallowed hard and were more forgiving to debtors—even to the extent of accepting substantial real losses—than at first expected. The IMF steadily grew in stature and authority.

But can these fragile arrangements continue indefinitely? Taken together, do the scrambling measures that averted calamity in the two years following August 1982 constitute the sort of overall reform needed to minimize the risk of disruption? Or, are the major reforms still ahead of us?

Increased lending and further rescheduling may offer some relief in the short run, but only if the borrowing country ultimately is able to back up its borrowing with long-term improvement in its economic performance. The trade surpluses by debtor countries in the last two years were helped by a strong U.S. dollar and the ability of the United States to run a gigantic trade deficit. But such trade surpluses cannot be sustained without general economic improvements in the borrowing countries. Otherwise, today's borrowing just adds to tomorrow's debt service. If that service is met by more borrowing, eventually confidence crumbles as the scheme takes on the appearance of a "Ponzi game" of explosively increasing debt.

Correspondingly, problem debtors have cut imports with a vengeance. Mexico's imports in 1983, for example, were 60 percent below their level of a year earlier. Beyond the short run, import restriction cannot be an enduring solution. The severe import cuts in debtor countries are provoking simultaneous surges in inflation and steep declines in output. As domestic austerity measures are put in place to control inflation, output will drop still further. Indeed, even if import cuts did not hurt the debtors' trading partners, the ultimate prosperity of the debtors depends, to a large extent, on continued imports. Without them, growth is far less likely.

The only way in which debtor nations will be able to resolve their financial problems while resuming growth is if they are able to increase their exports. Yet here a crucial variable emerges: what if problem debtors cannot gain needed access to the markets of industrialized countries?

This possibility raises the specter of a mutually reinforcing debt/trade crisis:

♦ A loss of confidence by lenders creates a balance of payments crunch for the high-debt LDCs. Attempting to cope with the shortfall, the LDCs try to push their exports as much as possible.

♦ The export drive of the LDCs increases pressure on labor-intensive, politically influential industries in advanced countries. These industries seek and receive protection.

♦ The bankers, seeing that debtors are having difficulty increasing their exports, become even less willing to lend. This increases balance of payments pressure and induces debtors to make further efforts to promote exports, and the cycle begins again.

Before long this process could lead to both a moratorium or repudiation of debt and a disruption of North-South trade.

U.S. Policy

Stakes. The United States has compelling stakes in avoiding a downward debt/trade spiral. On the broadest scale, the United States is concerned with safeguarding the stability of the international trade and financial regimes and ensuring that key multilateral institutions respond to the challenges. It is also in the U.S. interest to promote political stability within the debtor countries. Austerity, imposed from inside or out, undermines political and social cohesion.

More immediately, the LDC debt problem is important to the United States, because it potentially threatens the solvency of key U.S. banks (the nine largest U.S. banks have more than 100 percent of their equity exposed in Mexico, Brazil, and Argentina), the investments of major U.S. multinationals in the debtor countries and U.S. export markets. If America's private monetary, investment, and trade links with LDCs uncouple, more U.S. jobs will be lost, more banks could be threatened, and the prospect for sustaining economic recovery will diminish.

Policy Instruments. To be sure, the United States cannot stabilize the debt/trade relationship by itself. Any U.S. approach must take full account of the available financial, macroeconomic, and trade instruments:

- ♦ financial instruments—to take the pressure off by reducing the burden of debt service;
- ♦ macroeconomic instruments—to relieve the situation through lower interest rates and/or recovery;
- ♦ trade instruments—to help the LDCs increase their exports.

None of these instruments can work on its own. Together, however, they might nudge the situation toward resolution.

Financial Instruments. Official intervention could ease the problems of debtor countries in one of two ways. First, the short-run situation could be eased by increased official lending by governments or international institutions. Although the United States has so far opposed this approach, except to meet extraordinary problems on a case-by-case basis, increased official transfers would remove some of the immediate need for countries to cut imports and expand exports.

It may be possible to use the linkage between trade and financial policy to sell official lending politically. The more lending there is, of course, the more LDCs will be able to import from advanced countries, and the link can be made direct if the lending takes the form of export credits. One positive step in this direction is the increased willingness of the United States to expand the funds available through the Export-Import Bank and to use these funds in new, innovative ways. Other possibilities exist through such agencies as the Commodity Credit Corporation.

Clearly, the private sector has a major role to play. New investment would be as valuable to the debtor as new loans. If the LDC governments could credibly reassure foreign investors and if the industrialized country governments could find the political safety nets for would-be new investment, capital flows might be increased, and trade adjustment problems eased. Thus far, however, new multinational investment flows into the LDCs have slowed substantially.

Unless the improvement in debtor countries' trade balances is kept up, additional official lending will not provide a permanent solution. To achieve a purely financial solution to the debt problem, governments would have to go far beyond lending to a scheme of global debt restructuring such as those recently proposed by many observers. These schemes generally involve an official buy out of debt at some discount from par, followed by a restructuring of the debt into longer-term, lower-interest loans. Creditor country banks and governments would be forced to share the suffering of their borrowers by accepting real as opposed to paper losses.

Unless forced on the creditors by a perilous crisis, however, large-scale debt restructuring is extremely difficult to sell to governments and particularly to the U.S. Congress where a coalition of liberals and conservatives are suspicious of any move in this direction. In any event, it would be desirable to avoid this course of action if possible, because it would be seen as simultaneously bailing out the banks and the debtor countries and encouraging irresponsible borrowing and lending practices in the future.

In the long term or if the debt situation gets completely out of hand, large-scale debt restructuring may still be necessary. But if the economic recovery in the West remains strong and interest rates do not move significantly upward, then the much more modest option of some official lending, together with other policies, will be all that can be mounted and may be enough.

Macroeconomic Instruments. Both a sustained recovery in the industrial world and a reduction in interest rates would do a great deal to help the debtor countries. The recovery would boost their exports, while lower interest rates would reduce their debt service. The problem is how this can be engineered.

The industrialized countries could accelerate their economic recovery and temporarily lower interest rates by adopting more expansionary monetary policies. A turn to more expansionary money, however, would risk rekindling inflation and is thus a policy to be approached cautiously.

Alternatively, interest rates could be brought down by reducing budget deficits. The problem here is, of course, that the political will to do this is lacking.

In general, the macroeconomic policies that industrial countries might reasonably be expected to follow will not be significantly affected by the problems of the LDC debtors. These debtors would benefit from inflationary monetary policies, but these will not be undertaken for the debtors' sake alone. What could help the debtors is lower interest rates resulting from lower budget deficits—and these are in the interest of the advanced countries as well.

Trade Policy Instruments. A final route to relieving the pressure would be to use trade policy to help the LDC debtors increase their exports. At a minimum, advanced countries might forswear new protectionist actions that directly reduce the ability of countries with debt problems to earn foreign exchange.

More ambitiously, there could be a deliberate effort to provide special trade access for problem debtors. The use of the Strategic Petroleum Reserve as a funnel for official help for Mexico can be viewed as an example. Some specific policy possibilities are suggested below, but care will have to be taken to ensure that such policy initiatives do not disrupt the whole trade policy process.

For their part, debtor nations can manage their own policies in such a way as to minimize the trade frictions associated with the debt crisis. They cannot avoid the necessity of reducing imports and increasing exports, but the way in which they achieve these matters. The more that debtor countries rely on market mechanisms, such as exchange rate adjustment rather than subsidies and import restrictions, the less friction will be created. Furthermore, to the extent that import restrictions and export promoting actions are temporary, transparent, and consistent with accepted international trade practices, they are less likely to provoke protectionist retaliation from industrialized countries.

It is unrealistic to rely on the enlightened self-interest of the United States and its industrialized partners to keep their markets open to the LDC imports. If the U.S. Congress in particular is to support such market access, the LDCs may have to limit their export subsidies and adhere more fully to GATT rules.

Policy Options. Any effective U.S. policy must combine the instruments above. It is useful, however, to make a basic distinction between incremental options and bolder initiatives.

The pressures on the United States to opt for an incremental approach to managing debt/trade links are almost by definition overwhelming. The early success of the incremental approach that has served quite well for two years makes it difficult to envision a sharp change in policy approach in the absence of a systemic crisis. As so far practiced, the incremental approach involves the provision of additional liquidity to debtor nations, sustained recovery not only in the United States but throughout the industrial world, and continued access of the LDC exports to industrialized country markets. Banks would need to continue to provide new money and roll over existing debts in response to success in debtor country austerity programs. The IMF would remain a vigilant, powerful watchdog, assuring economic discipline in debtor countries and continued participation by international banks. These conditions, if allowed to take hold, could turn a vicious circle of trade and debt into a virtuous circle.

If all goes well, as the exports of debtors increase, their financial position will ease. As their balance of payments position improves, extraordinary measures of export promotion will become less neces-

34

sary, which in turn will ease protectionist pressures. Exports will improve further, lender and investor confidence will revive, and the crisis will fade away. For such an incremental approach to "solve" the long-term debt situation, debtors will need to keep their economies in line, creditor countries will need to resist protectionist demands from those sectors pummeled by the LDC exports and continue to run substantial trade deficits, banks will need to forgo profits and accept some losses on their LDC lending, while bank supervisors provide help as needed.

A major departure from current practice flows from the premise that despite initial success in holding back the flood waters, an incremental approach will be inadequate. Specifically, a heavy infusion of funds underwritten by the central banks of the industrialized countries and still more forgiveness and loss by the banks may be required to avert a major collapse. This increase in public and private support would hinge on long-term debtor commitments to liberalize trade restrictions.

That the debt problem is not behind us is clear. The strong dollar, although it helped promote the LDC exports and discourage the LDC imports, also has made servicing their dollar-denominated debt more costly. If, and when, the dollar drops from its dizzying levels, the servicing of the debts will prove easier, but the LDC trade situation almost certainly will erode. Similarly, if inflation reignites in the United States and interest rates go up instead of down, the LDC situation could worsen quickly and tragically. One sign that there is still a potential for disaster is Citibank's purchase of $900 million in insurance on its LDC loans in September 1984. In part, this was a shrewd move by Citibank to insure roughly three-fourths of their critical LDC exposure at a reasonable price. But at the same time, if Citibank, the bank that has most steadfastly argued that there is no serious danger of default, repudiation, or financial collapse takes such precautions, others might become wary.

As of early 1985, the prospect for bold, nonincremental change in the absence of a giant new flare-up of the debt situation looks remote. Creditors, debtors, and the IMF have become used to working out individual countries' problems. National regulators have tightened their supervision of international lending. Banks have reexamined their own internal lending policies to avoid blundering into a repetition of their earlier mistakes. Everyone hopes that these important actions coupled with global recovery will be enough to make it unnecessary to turn the entire financial structure on its head. As a result, there is at present strong resistance in the industrialized countries to increased financing for the debtors at either market or discretionary rates. At the same time, the debtors may be unwilling and perhaps incapable of making further concessions needed to reassure central and private bankers of their renewed creditworthiness.

Exchange Rates and Trade

As an institutional matter, the management of exchange rates and the conduct of trade policy are separate. As a matter of political reality, however, there always has been a close link between exchange rates and trade issues. In the United States, in particular, the politics of trade are strongly conditioned by the exchange rate. When the dollar has been strong, as in the late 1960s, the mid-1970s and the early 1980s, concern about foreign competition has been high; when the dollar has been weak as in the late 1970s, free trade has commanded more support.

Since 1980, the U.S. dollar has experienced an extraordinary appreciation against all other major currencies. This rise in the dollar has raised dramatically the costs of U.S. producers relative to their foreign competitors. What makes the situation particularly difficult is that this recent loss of U.S. competitiveness has been overlaid on a longer-term structural problem involving the value of the Japanese yen.

The Setting

The Recent Strength of the Dollar. From 1980 to the fourth quarter of 1983, the U.S. dollar rose by 68 percent against the French franc, 38 percent against the German mark, and 15 percent against the Japanese yen. The universality of this rise—the dollar rose against every major currency—shows that the rise was a case of a "strong dollar" rather than a "weak franc" or "weak yen." That is, the causes of the change in exchange rates must be sought in U.S. policies and events rather than in the actions of foreign countries.

The sources of the strong dollar are not hard to find. U.S. macroeconomic policy in the last few years has been characterized by a conflict between monetary and fiscal policy. On one side, the Federal Reserve has remained dedicated to fighting inflation. First it imposed the most severe recession since the 1930s, and now it is tightening money to prevent the recovery from proceeding at a rate that could restart inflation. On the other side, Congress and the administration have cut taxes without corresponding cuts in spending, producing a strong fiscal stimulus to the economy. The combination of these factors drove interest rates to unprecedented levels in 1981 and has kept these rates from falling much despite the dramatic decline in inflation. High interest rates in the United States, in turn, have attracted inflows of foreign capital, keeping the dollar strong despite a growing U.S. trade deficit.

The crucial linkage, then, is from U.S. monetary and fiscal policies to interest rates, then to capital inflows. Any policy to bring the dollar down must either change the fundamental macroeconomic policies, block the inflows of capital, or offset them in some way.

The effects of the strong dollar also are quite clear. The United States had a record trade deficit in 1983 and an even larger deficit in 1984. Econometric estimates suggest that much of the increase in the trade deficit can be attributed to the strength of the dollar. The fact that the source of the deficit lies in financial factors, however, will not prevent political demands for a trade policy response.

Although the loss of U.S. competitiveness has been general, the flash point of the political pressure is in U.S. trade with Japan. In this trade there is a problem that goes beyond the recent strength of the dollar— for even before the dollar's rise Japan was perceived by many businessmen to have an excessive competitive advantage.

The Persistent Weakness of the Yen. Comparisons of production costs suggest that Japanese manufacturers only would be on a level with their foreign competitors if the yen were at an exchange rate of 200 to the dollar or less. Yet even before its recent slide, the value of the yen was persistently below this level. Table 1 shows the "real" or inflation-adjusted exchange rate of the yen against the dollar from 1973 to 1982, adjusted to 1982 prices. The table shows that in only two years, 1978 and 1979, did the yen reach the levels that many businesses— including some Japanese—believe would produce a rough equality of costs between Japanese and U.S. manufacturing.

The persistent Japanese surplus in trade in manufactures corresponds to this persistent cost advantage for Japanese producers. In 1981 Japan's exports of manufactures were worth four times its imports. The Japanese trade surplus in manufactured goods was roughly 10 percent of Japan's gross national product (GNP), and more than 20 percent of Japan's value-added in industry.

Why has Japanese industry had this persistent cost advantage? There have been many allegations that the Japanese government deliberately has tried to hold down the value of the yen, but no evidence has been found. The most obvious interference of the Japanese government with the balance of payments has been restrictions on capital outflow— restrictions that tend to strengthen rather than weaken it.

TABLE 1

Real Exchange Rate of the Yen against the Dollar, Adjusted to 1982 Prices

1973	257
1974	246
1975	245
1976	236
1977	211
1978	171
1979	192
1980	209
1981	213
1982	249
Avg. 1973–1982	223

TABLE 2

Trade Balances, United States and Japan, 1981 ($ billions)

	United States	Japan
Manufactures	+5	+118
Primary products	−50	−105
Services	+39	−14

In any case, we need not try to find an explanation in Japanese policy, because there is another explanation that is sufficient. The persistent weakness of the yen is explained by the fact that Japan's surplus in manufacturing is offset by deficits elsewhere in the balance of payments. Japan's balance on merchandise trade as a whole has been only moderately in surplus; and Japan runs a deficit on trade in services. So, the overall surplus on current account over the 1973 to 1981 period was no larger than that of the United States.

Table 2 shows a comparison of the structure of the United States and Japanese balance of trade in 1981. The difference is striking. The United States was able to offset much of its oil import bill with agricultural exports, so the balance of trade in primary products was only a moderate deficit, largely offset by the U.S. surplus in services. Japan, by contrast, ran a huge deficit in primary products, and a deficit in services as well. The surplus in manufactures did not exert upward pressure on the yen, because, despite its size, it was only barely enough to offset these deficits in other areas.

The explanation for the persistent weakness of the yen, then, lies in the fact that Japan is poor in natural resources and has few service exports. These factors keep the yen weak despite the competitive advantage of Japan's manufactures. Or to put it another way, Japan must have a competitive advantage in manufacturing to offset its weakness elsewhere.

Policy Implications. The analysis presented here suggests that the problem posed by exchange rates for trade policy is really two separate problems. The first of these is the problem of the strong dollar, which is a multilateral issue. The second is the persistent weakness of the yen.

Dealing with the linkage between exchange rates and trade policy is therefore a twofold task. The first part of the task is to bring the dollar down—something that is easy in theory, but that requires political will that may not be available. The second task is to find a way for Japan to pay for its raw material imports without disrupting the trading system—a task of extreme difficulty.

Bringing Down the Dollar: U.S. Policy Options

The strong dollar essentially reflects the combined effects of loose financial and tight monetary policies in the United States, which drive up U.S. interest rates and attract foreign capital. There are four basic ways in which the United States and other countries could try to weaken the dollar. First, governments could attempt to offset capital inflows by selling dollars and buying other currencies on the foreign exchange market. Second, an attempt could be made to limit the capital inflows through capital controls—either controls on capital inflows by the United States or controls on outflows by other countries such as Japan. Third, the United States could follow a more expansionary monetary policy. Fourth, the United States could reduce its budget deficit.

Each of these options has problems. Either the option is of doubtful effectiveness, or it has undesirable side effects, or it is politically difficult to swallow. If anything is to be done, there will have to be a political willingness to make hard choices.

Exchange Market Intervention. To weaken the dollar, central banks could sell dollars and buy other currencies on the foreign exchange market. In fact, they have already done so to a considerable extent. For example, Japan sold nearly $10 billion during 1982 in an attempt to arrest the yen's slide. European countries also have sold dollars in an effort to support their currencies; and in August 1983 the United States began making modest purchases of foreign currency to stabilize "disorderly" markets.

The problem with exchange market intervention as a solution to the strong dollar is that all the evidence suggests that it is ineffective. If the fundamentals of interest differentials and expectations about the future make foreign investors want to invest in the United States, an intervention can have only a limited impact on the exchange rate. Suppose, for example, that a sale of dollars by a central bank depresses the dollar. If the underlying factors behind dollar strength are unchanged, the cheapening of the dollar will encourage foreigners to buy even more U.S. assets, offsetting the effects of the intervention. Most studies of the evidence—including the international study performed after the Versailles Summit—have found that intervention is ineffective at anything beyond some day-to-day smoothing of exchange market movements. In particular, intervention by itself cannot appreciably alter large, sustained movements such as the rise of the dollar against the yen, the mark, and most other currencies.

Capital Controls. The reason why intervention is ineffective is that in a world of integrated capital markets any intervention is likely to be swamped by private capital movements in the opposite direction. This suggests that to be effective in altering exchange rates, governments might attempt to limit these capital flows. In particular, the dollar might be weakened either if the United States imposed restrictions on inflows of capital or if Japan and other countries imposed restrictions on outflows.

There are two problems with this as a policy option. First, it may not be practical. Second, it may not be desirable.

It is hard to believe that the United States could impose effective controls on capital inflows without disrupting the role of the United States as the world's banker. There are many channels through which capital can flow into the United States, and many of them are difficult to monitor. The United States both imports capital, typically at the short end of the maturity spectrum, and exports capital, typically through long-term lending and direct foreign investment. Thus any effort to limit capital inflows would probably disrupt the financial intermediation business of U.S. banks and be frustrated by an offsetting decline in capital outflows.

Prospects are better for an imposition of capital outflow controls by other countries. Japan, in particular, with its more centralized economic system, might be able to impose effective limits on its export of capital. The Japanese,however, are unwilling to do this—for the simple reason that they have recently liberalized their regulations for export of capital under U.S. pressure. This pressure reflected complaints by U.S. businesses, many of them the same firms that now complain about the weakness of the yen.

It is also far from clear whether a limitation of capital flows to the United States is actually in U.S. interests. The combination of fiscal and monetary policies has led to rising interest rates in the United States, but inflows of foreign capital have helped limit that rise. If we were to cut off those inflows, interest rates would rise even higher, deterring investment. Although a weaker dollar would help the trade balance, it is hard to make an economic case that the trade-off of a better trade balance for higher interest rates and lower investment is a desirable one.

Nonetheless, there is a political case for making the trade-off. The strength of the dollar is creating severe strains on the international trading system; if that system is disrupted, it may be impossible to reconstruct. It may be better to endure high interest rates and depressed investment for a time rather than risk a permanent collapse of the open trading system.

But it would be far better to do neither. To avoid the unpleasant choices involved in capital controls, however, requires a fundamental shift in monetary or fiscal policy.

Monetary Policy. There is no question that a loosening of U.S. monetary policy could temporarily lower interest rates and drive the dollar down. The question is whether it is a good idea to do this given the side effects.

The problem is that an expansionary U.S. monetary policy would risk a renewed surge in inflation. The U.S. money supply recently has been growing much faster than would be sustainable for long without high inflation, and the economy has made a rapid recovery from recession. To pursue an even more expansionary policy would be to take a real risk of throwing away the gains made against inflation in the last three years.

It is possible that these risks are actually not great. Inflation has remained low during the recovery, and there is a respectable case to be made against the Federal Reserve's recent tightening of policy. But the kind of monetary expansion required to drive down the dollar enough to make much of a difference to U.S. competitiveness almost surely would be inflationary.

The fundamental problem is that any noninflationary monetary policy will be associated with a strong dollar as long as fiscal policy remains out of control.

Fiscal Policy. The key to the problem of the strong dollar is the U.S. fiscal deficit. This deficit absorbs most of U.S. net savings, driving up interest rates, attracting foreign capital, and keeping the dollar high. As long as the deficit remains high, all policy options for bringing the dollar down either will be ineffective or will involve trading one evil for another. Intervention will not work; capital controls will drive interest rates still higher; monetary expansion will be inflationary.

If the deficit could be brought under control, by contrast, the other options would not be needed. Lower government demands for credit would translate into lower interest rates and a lower dollar.

Bringing down the deficit, then, is clearly the most desirable policy option. The only problem is that there is no sign that anyone is willing to make the necessary sacrifices.

The Persistent Weakness of the Yen: Policy Options

Even if the forces that have driven the dollar to its current high level can be reversed, there will still be a yen problem. Japan's dependence on imported raw materials still will keep the yen depressed, giving its manufacturers a cost advantage over competitors.

In an ideal world, Japan's surplus in manufactures trade would not be regarded as a problem. Japan may sell more manufactures to the United States than it buys in return, but it also buys U.S. food, lumber, and so on. Even if Japan buys its raw materials in the rest of the world, this creates purchasing power that can be used to buy U.S. exports. There is no purely economic reason why the world cannot run smoothly with a huge Japanese export surplus in manufactured goods, and no purely economic reason why trade between any pair of countries must be balanced.

But there are increasing political difficulties in sustaining this position. The fragile political coalition behind free trade is built on the basis of an expectation of mutual gain to producers. U.S. business and labor have backed free trade (to the extent they have), because they have been convinced that increased imports will be matched by increased exports. This is still true; but in the case of Japan the linkage between imports and exports is too indirect to carry much political weight. As long as Japan runs a huge surplus in manufactures trade with other industrial countries, the manufacturing sectors of these countries will feel that they are being hurt.

There are no easy answers to this problem. Unless huge reserves of oil are discovered off the coast of Japan, Japan will continue to have to export far more manufactures than it imports. The only two policy options that seem to be available are protection against Japan's exports, which could have disastrous consequences, or a commitment to the principle of free trade rather than to particular outcomes, which may not be politically practical.

Protectionism and the Yen: A Vicious Circle? The politically easiest response to the Japanese trade surplus in manufactures is to limit Japanese exports. A substantial part of Japan's trade is already covered by "voluntary" restraint agreements, and there have been proposals to set explicit limits on the bilateral surplus Japan will be allowed to have with the United States. So far, the response of the governments of other industrial countries to Japan's manufacturing surplus basically has been to give ground slowly to the demands for protection.

Aside from the question of its desirability, however, this response ultimately must be self-defeating. The interaction of trade policy with the value of the yen will turn protectionism into a downward spiral with no bottom.

The essential point is that to pay for its raw material imports, Japan must run an export surplus in manufactures of roughly $100 billion. If other countries refuse to accept a trade deficit in some particular sector, the Japanese surplus will simply manifest itself somewhere else. The way this will work is through the exchange rate. Suppose, for example, that Europe protects against some set of Japanese exports. The effect will be to weaken the yen, leading to an increased Japanese trade surplus elsewhere—both in other sectors of Japanese-European trade and in trade with other countries, such as the United States.

It is easy to see how this can lead to a vicious circle. It may be that the rest of the world is essentially unwilling to accept the size of Japan's surplus in manufactures. Countries will begin by protecting the industries that feel most threatened by Japanese competition, but as the yen weakens, other sectors will become equally threatened; when these in turn are protected, the yen will fall still further, creating pressure on additional sectors and so on.

It is important to note both the international and the interindustry spillovers in this process. Because Japan must sell somewhere, European protectionism increases the pressure on U.S. industry and vice versa. For the same reason, restricting Japanese exports in one industry increases the pressure on others. If Japanese steel and auto exports are to be restricted, it would not be surprising to see Japan competing in tractors and computers.

In the end, unless Japan's economy is to be strangled for lack of export markets, protectionist measures cannot provide an answer to the problem of the yen. Instead, some way must be found to live with the Japanese surplus in manufactured goods. The only way this can happen is through a major change both in the reality of Japan's trade policy and in the way this reality is perceived elsewhere.

The Role of Japanese Policy. The problem of Japan's trade surplus in manufactures would be a difficult one even if Japan followed unobjectionable policies itself. What makes it critical is the fact that Japan's own trade policy is one that increases international tensions.

It is easy to understand why Japan continues to pursue policies of protection and industrial targeting. A mercantilist tradition of government involvement in the economy is still deeply embedded. Furthermore, the dependence of Japan on imported raw materials makes it difficult for government officials to trust the market and let the trade balance take care of itself.

Given the realities of the situation, however, an interventionist international trade policy is exactly the wrong response for Japan. As an island nation dependent on imported raw materials and requiring access to export markets for her manufactures, Japan—like nineteenth century Britain—depends upon an open world trading system. To preserve that system, however, Japan itself would have to become an exemplar of openness.

The best chance for coping with the problem of Japan's persistent trade surplus in manufacturing would be for Japan to make a clearcut, dramatic shift toward more liberal trade policies. This would not eliminate the surplus—regardless of its trade policies, Japan will still end up exporting many more manufactured goods than it imports. But a Japan that could claim credibly to have clean hands would be able to take advantage of the considerable support that remains for the principle of free trade.

The United States and the New Technological Competition

by
Stephen A. Merrill

Last year a wave of imports erased the traditional U.S. trade surplus in high technology goods. This astonishing reversal occurred over only four years and gained momentum only in the last two. From its peak of $25.5 billion in 1980, the trade balance slipped to $22.0 billion in 1982, to $17.0 billion in 1983, and plunged into negative numbers in the second half of 1984. Thus has the most reliable if not the largest offset to perennial U.S. deficits in low technology manufactures and oil at least temporarily disappeared. (See table 1.)[1]

To be sure, the sudden collapse of the U.S. high technology trade position that has occurred almost entirely on the import side of the ledger derives mainly from two sources of imports— Japan and the NICs of East Asia—and is heavily concentrated in communications equipment and electronic components. Between 1982 and 1983 the high technology deficit with Japan jumped 38 percent from $6.3 billion to $8.7 billion. With South Korea, Taiwan, Hong Kong, and Singapore, the deficit nearly doubled, from $1.3 billion to $2.4 billion. (See table 2.) The $3 billion increase in the communications equipment and components deficit (from $4.3 billion to $7.2 billion) represented fully 60 percent of the overall decline in the high technology trade balance. (See table 3.) On the export side, the United States lost ground in Latin American markets that were growing rapidly until the debt crisis; but modest export gains elsewhere, including increased sales to Japan, more than compensated for these losses.

It is also the case, however, that total U.S. high technology exports have ceased to grow since 1981. Further, the five-fold increase in U.S. exports from 1970 to 1980 masks a simultaneous decline in U.S. high technology export share overall and in most product categories. The high technology share of U.S. imports of manufactures increased gradually through the 1970s, as did high technology imports as a proportion of exports.

The United States, as a result, faces an unprecedented competitive challenge to its leadership in industries of greatest strength and in the

45

TABLE 1

U.S. Trade in High Technology[1] and Non-High Technology Manufactures, 1970–1983 (General Imports, c.i.f.; Domestic exports, f.a.s.)

| | Value (Billions of dollars) | | | | | | High Technology Share (In percent) | | | |
| | High Technology | | | Non-High Technology | | | Total U.S. | | U.S. Manufactures | |
	Exports[2]	Imports	Balance	Exports	Imports	Balance	Exports	Imports	Exports	Imports
1970	10.3e	4.2e	6.1e	19.0e	22.8e	−3.8e	24.2e	9.8e	35.2e	15.6e
1971	11.4e	4.9e	6.5e	19.0e	27.4e	−8.4e	26.2e	10.0e	37.5e	15.2e
1972	11.9e	6.3e	5.6e	21.8e	33.7e	−11.9e	24.3e	10.6e	35.3e	15.8e
1973	15.9e	7.9e	8.0e	28.8e	39.8e	−11.0e	22.6e	10.6e	35.6e	16.6e
1974	21.5	9.8e	11.7e	42.0	49.7e	−7.7e	22.1	8.8e	33.9	16.4e
1975	22.9	9.5e	13.4e	48.1	45.5e	+2.6e	21.5	9.0e	32.4	17.3e
1976	25.6	13.2e	12.4e	51.6	56.4e	−4.8e	22.5	10.0e	33.2	19.0e
1977	27.3	15.3e	12.0e	52.9	66.6e	−13.7e	22.9	9.5e	34.0	18.7e
1978	33.9	20.1	13.8	60.6	86.7	−26.1	24.0	10.8	35.9	18.8
1979	42.3	22.5	19.8	74.3	96.3	−22.0	23.7	10.1	36.3	18.9
1980	53.2	27.7	25.5	90.7	103.8	−13.1	24.6	10.8	37.0	21.1
1981	58.5	33.5	25.0	95.8	115.5	−19.7	25.6	12.3	37.9	22.5
1982	56.2	34.2	22.0	83.5	116.1	−32.6	27.1	13.4	40.2	22.8
1983	57.9	40.9	17.0	74.5	129.7	−55.2	29.6	15.2	43.7	24.0
Jan–June 1983	30.0[3]	18.5	11.5							
Jan–June 1984	31.4[3]	27.7	3.7							

[1] U.S. Department of Commerce DOC-3 definition
[2] Excludes special category exports
[3] Includes domestic and foreign exports, f.a.s.
e: Estimated

Source: U.S. Department of Commerce, Bureau of the Census.

TABLE 2
U.S. High Technology[1] Trade by Region (Billions of dollars)

	EEC(10)			Canada			Japan		
	exports[2]	imports[3]	balance	exports[2]	imports[3]	balance	exports[2]	imports[3]	balance
1978	10.0	4.3	5.7	3.9	1.6	2.3	2.3	6.9	−4.6
1979	13.0	4.9	8.1	4.7	2.1	2.6	3.4	6.8	−3.4
1980	17.1	6.7	10.4	5.4	2.8	2.6	4.0	7.7	−3.7
1981	17.5	7.3	10.2	6.6	3.6	3.0	4.8	10.6	−5.8
1982	16.4	6.9	9.5	6.1	3.4	2.7	4.8	11.1	−6.3
1983	17.2	7.3	9.9	6.7	3.5	3.2	5.6	14.3	−8.7
Jan–June 1984	9.6	4.9	4.7	4.1	2.5	1.6	2.9	10.2	−7.3

	East Asian NICS			Major Latin American Countries		
	exports[2]	imports[3]	balance	exports[2]	imports[3]	balance
1978	2.4	3.5	−1.1	2.9	1.2	1.7
1979	3.6	4.0	−0.4	4.4	1.5	2.9
1980	4.5	4.6	−0.1	5.9	1.7	4.2
1981	4.3	5.4	−1.1	6.8	2.0	4.8
1982	4.5	5.8	−1.3	4.7	2.0	2.7
1983	5.7	8.1	−2.4	4.2	2.5	1.7
Jan–June 1984	3.0	5.2	−2.2	2.2	1.5	0.7

[1]DOC-3 definition
[2]Domestic and foreign exports, f.a.s.
[3]General imports, c.i.f.
Source: U.S. Department of Commerce: ITA, Bureau of the Census.

TABLE 3

U.S. Trade Balances in Selected High Technology[1] Products (Billions of dollars)

	1978	1979	1980	1981	1982	1983	1984 (Jan–June)
Guided Missiles and Spacecraft	0.6	0.6	0.7	0.6	1.1	1.0	0.5
Communications Equipment and Electronic Components	-2.8	-2.3	-1.9	-3.8	-4.3	-7.2	-5.9
Aircraft and Parts	8.3	9.6	11.9	13.2	10.8	12.0	4.5
Office Computing and Accounting Machines	2.9	4.1	6.1	6.8	6.3	5.4	1.9
Ordnance and Accessories	0.4	0.5	0.5	0.5	0.5	0.8	0.4
Drugs and Medicines	0.7	0.8	1.0	1.2	1.3	1.2	0.5
Industrial Inorganic Chemicals	0.2	0.6	0.5	0.6	0.6	0.4	-0.07
Professional and Scientific Instruments	0.7	1.4	1.6	1.3	1.6	0.8	-0.03
Engines, Turbines and Parts	1.7	2.0	1.9	1.9	2.0	1.5	0.5
Plastics, Synthetic Resins, Rubber, etc.	1.7	3.3	4.2	4.2	3.6	3.0	1.4

[1]DOC-3 definition.
Source: U.S. Department of Commerce: ITA and Bureau of the Census.

technologies that will contribute to the revival of mature manufacturing industries, the continued growth and competitiveness of much of the service sector, and further productivity advances in agriculture. This challenge is not strictly a phenomenon of the early 1980s and will not greatly diminish under any foreseeable economic conditions.

Facing a prolonged period of uncertain growth prospects, severe dislocations in basic industries, and fierce competition for world markets, the industrial countries have come to regard their ability to exploit advances in technology as vital to their economic futures. Their attention has focused on the same few technologies and industries, primarily in the information sector, computer-driven and integrated manufacturing processes, industrial materials, aircraft and aerospace, and microbiology. With increasing sophistication, certain of their governments are using an array of public instruments to shape a national comparative advantage in high technologies. These efforts are unlikely to be deterred.

The newly industrializing countries have greatly expanded manufacture for export of standardized but increasingly sophisticated products, especially electronic equipment and devices. This growth is a function of both indigenous and foreign investment, the latter attracted by lower labor costs and other inducements. The new capacity and the relative cost advantages it reflects will endure for a considerable time, and the ease of transferring production know-how will enable these countries to continue to move into progressively higher value-added manufacturing.

Obviously, the domestic economic recovery has not removed the challenge and in some respects exacerbates it. In the near term, the inordinately high value of the dollar, differences in growth rates, and the austerity policies of Latin American countries burdened by enormous debts mean rising imports and depressed exports. From a somewhat longer perspective, the costs of prolonged stagflation and the methods used to combat it have been great for industries dependent upon maintaining a high rate of innovation and access to foreign markets. Recovery, although critical to high technology companies, will not enable them to recoup lost investment opportunities and sales; and projected federal budget deficits and the uncertainty of capital inflows complicate the investment picture for the foreseeable future. Japan and other emerging competitors, in the meantime, have managed to sustain higher overall savings and investment rates and lower capital costs, inflation, and interest rates along with weaker currencies. Inevitably, these differences will play themselves out over a period of several years.

The traditional response of government to competitive pressures in circumstances less critical to vital interests than these is to protect threatened industries. But aside from the fact that import relief rarely improves competitiveness, resort to the trade remedy laws has several distinct drawbacks in the area of high technology. The statutes for the most part do not address restrictions on foreign market access, where trade problems generally first appear. The complaint process is expensive and time-consuming; and relief is confined to a narrow, current product line. Because innovation can abruptly change what products are critical to an industry's or company's success in international competition, import relief may lose much of its value before it is granted. High technology industries, moreover, are particularly vulnerable to retaliation, not only because our chief suppliers are also our major markets but also because these industries are typically multinational.[2]

The alternative of emulating our competitors, primarily Japan, is commonly, and, on the whole, correctly dismissed but without serious analysis. The question should be, "imitate what?" Appeals to replace our "adversarial" with their "cooperative" public-private sector relations are widely echoed but are meaningless without specific recommendations beyond the creation of a new forum for interest group accommodation. Often overlooked in these comparisons are major structural differences, such as the close relationships between banks and corporations and macroeconomic policies heavily biased toward industrial investment, that go far toward explaining Japan's economic performance. To adopt these, however, would entail radical changes in our way of doing business and in patterns of consumer consumption. Extensive government intervention to give U.S. industries advantages comparable to those enjoyed by their competitors would be at odds with the nation's prevailing market-oriented philosophy.

To craft an effective response to the competitive challenge in high technology is to follow a largely uncharted path—not one the United States has traveled in the past nor one already cleared by foreign competitors. To accomplish this task requires a clear appraisal of U.S. stakes, assets, and liabilities, the threats posed, legitimately or illegitimately, by trading partners, and the advantages and disadvantages of the policy instruments available.

U.S. Stakes and Performance

The U.S. economy is emerging from a decade or longer of slow or negative economic and productivity growth; high unemployment, inflation, and interest rates; repeated trade deficits of unprecedented proportions; and wrenching dislocations in basic industries. The strong recovery has at least temporarily reversed the trends in economic growth and productivity, and monetary policy has sharply reduced inflation. Nevertheless, unemployment and real interest rates remain high; the trade deficit balloons; and automobiles, steel, machine tools, and other industries face another decade at least of adjustment. It is in this context that comparisons of sectors' performance during the last decade best illustrate the nation's economic stakes in its high technology industries:

- ◆ The output of high technology industries grew at twice the rate of U.S. industrial output as a whole.
- ◆ The average annual rate of price increases in the high technology sector was one-third that of the country's overall average inflation.
- ◆ The average annual growth in employment in high technology and its supporting industries exceeded the growth rate of total business employment by more than 50 percent.
- ◆ The average annual productivity growth rate in high technology was six times the average growth rate of U.S. business as a whole.
- ◆ U.S. high technology exports invariably exceeded imports by a substantial margin, although with few exceptions the U.S. registered trade deficits in all other types of manufactured goods. High technology exports are approaching one-half of all U.S. exports of manufactures.[3]

The continued growth of the high technology sector is neither assured nor is it an economic panacea. Technology-intensive industries will continue to employ a relatively small proportion of the nation's work force and, because of skill and wage differences, high capital-labor ratios, and international mobility, they will not absorb a great many of those entering the labor market or displaced from jobs in smokestack industries. But advances in robotics, computer-aided design, and automated manufacturing systems are beginning to transform the factory, whether engaged in mass production or in small-batch manufacturing, not only by cutting labor costs and boosting productivity but also by expanding product range and improving quality control. Similarly, the service sector, often considered a drag on overall worker productivity and a leading source of inflation, will achieve major efficiencies with accelerating application of computers, word processing equipment, and telecommunications systems. At least as revolutionary, though perhaps not as imminent, are the varied applications of the techniques collectively known as biotechnology —in the production of drugs,

51

chemicals, energy sources, and food plants with enhanced disease-resistance or nitrogen-fixing capabilities.

U.S. deterrence strategy relies on deployment of qualitatively superior weapon systems to offset the numerical advantage of opposing strategic and conventional forces, and the viability of current approaches to arms control hinges on sophisticated methods of verifying weapons limitations. Many basic military capabilities and some important dual use technologies—nuclear weapons, ballistic and cruise missiles, jet aircraft, radar, and numerically controlled machine tools— evolved in the context of military research and development. In recent years, however, the commercial market has excelled in new technology development and become a prime source of innovations in weapon system components, manufacturing methods and materials, and military command, communications, and intelligence. Across a broad spectrum of leading technologies —semiconductors, computer sciences, communications networks, lasers, new materials, and robotics—applications to weapon design and production typically lag behind commercial uses. Thus civilian technological innovation has a crucial bearing on national security and not merely through its contributions to growth, employment, and productivity that underlie a healthy economy capable of sustaining a strong defense posture.

From all of these perspectives it is therefore of concern that, by any of several measures of technology intensity, the United States was losing market share in a range of high technology industries well before the 1981-1983 dollar appreciation and the 1983 U.S. economic recovery. According to a Department of Commerce analysis, the U.S. share of industrial country high technology exports dropped 4.4 percent between 1970 and 1980. The losses were greatest in aircraft (12.9 percent), electronic components (12.2 percent), and jet engines (8.4 percent). Only in computers did the United States significantly increase its export share (by 4.0 percent).[4] As expected, the gains, apart from those in aircraft, jet engines, and drugs, accrued overwhelmingly to Japan. Continental Western Europe more or less held its own in most product groups. (See table 4.)

The best that has been made of these trends is that they are inevitable, irreversible, and on the whole benign. This rationalization has taken two forms, one premised on the peculiar circumstances of the industrial democracies following World War II, the other derived from international trade theory. The historical argument maintains that European and Japanese technological capabilities were bound to revive and partially erode the United States' unnatural postwar dominance. Product-cycle theory holds that a U.S. competitive advantage

52

TABLE 4

Comparative Changes in World (OECD) Export Shares by Commodity Group from 1970 to 1980 (In percent)

Commodity Group	United States			Japan			West Germany			France		
	1970	1980	Change from 1970–1980	1970	1980	Change from 1970–1980	1970	1980	Change from 1970–1980	1970	1980	Change from 1970–1980
Total merchandise trade	15.4	12.0	−3.4	8.9	10.6	+1.7	15.7	15.6	−0.1	8.1	9.0	+0.9
Manufactures (total)	18.4	16.4	−2.0	8.9	11.0	+2.1	19.8	19.8	0.0	9.1	10.2	+1.1
Technology-intensive products[1]	23.1	19.9	−3.2	9.7	14.5	+4.8	20.4	19.3	−1.1	7.6	9.0	+1.4
High-technology products[2]	28.8	24.4	−4.4	11.6	15.6	+4.0	16.5	16.1	−0.4	7.5	7.9	+0.4
Drugs and medicinals	17.1	15.8	−1.3	2.7	2.3	−0.4	19.9	17.6	−2.3	9.3	11.6	+2.3
Business machines and equipment	37.7	37.0	−0.7	8.0	9.9	+1.9	15.1	13.0	−2.1	7.8	7.8	0.0
Computers	31.5	35.5	+4.0	11.1	12.3	+1.2	11.2	12.1	+0.9	9.0	7.1	−1.9

TABLE 4 (continued)

Electrical and electronic machines and equipment	21.6	18.0	−3.6	10.3	18.7	+8.4	19.5	18.7	−0.8	8.1	9.2	+1.1
Telecommunications equipment	21.9	18.1	−3.8	11.9	23.1	+11.2	15.2	14.6	−0.6	5.5	7.7	+2.2
Electronic components	39.8	27.6	−12.2	6.3	27.0	+20.7	12.5	14.3	+1.8	8.6	8.8	+0.2
Consumer electronics	9.3	9.9	+0.6	49.0	53.0	+4.0	14.3	12.0	−2.3	2.3	5.5	+2.2
Jet engines	40.4	32.0	−8.4	0.1	0.1	0.0	5.4	5.3	−0.1	5.6	7.8	+2.2
Aircraft	66.0	53.1	−12.9	0.8	0.4	−0.4	2.9	10.7	+7.8	7.6	9.1	+1.5
Scientific instruments	29.3	26.8	−2.5	8.7	10.4	+1.7	21.5	19.4	−2.1	7.1	8.1	+1.0
Technology-intensive other than high technology products	20.8	17.7	−3.1	7.5	13.1	+5.6	22.4	20.9	−1.5	7.9	9.7	+1.8

[1]Technology-intensive products are produced by industries in which spending on R&D is 5 percent or more of gross product (BEA concept of value added) and/or "natural" scientists, engineers, and technicians comprise 5 percent or more of total employment.
[2]High-technology products are produced by industries in which spending on R&D is 10 percent or more of gross product (value added) and/or "natural" scientists, engineers, and technicians comprise 10 percent or more of total employment.
Source: U.S. Department of Commerce, compiled from individual country data reported to the United Nations.

in technology-intensive manufactures is usually temporary because, as processes become routinized and transferrable, production gravitates to economies affording lower factor costs. From either perspective, increased specialization and a steady stream of innovation may be all that are necessary to sustain a U.S. advantage and a net export position.

Inevitable or not, the development of free world economies and technical capacity has long been an objective of U.S. policy, benefiting U.S. exports and strengthening Western security arrangements. Although these purposes continue to have validity, two concerns remain. The first, revealed by the trade statistics, is the breadth of the predominantly Asian competitive challenge. In the 1970s U.S. high technology producers far outperformed the economy as a whole. That in the same period by a standard measure they managed to increase their world market share in only one major product category while losing ground in all others underscores their vulnerability.

The second concern is the emergence of stiff competition, primarily but not exclusively Japanese, in a number of technologically advanced products and processes that are submerged or yet to be reflected in aggregated data. The most publicized examples are the Japanese dominance of the merchant market in random access memory (RAM) components of computers, the elimination of the U.S. monopoly in commercial jet aircraft by the European consortium Airbus Industrie, and the entry of the Japanese into the small but important market for ultra-high speed computers. Concern has also been expressed about Japanese advances in optical fibers, biological process engineering, programmable automation, industrial ceramics, and other emerging or keystone technologies.

None of these cases represents a clear-cut example of foreign technological supremacy translated into dominant market share. In several instances—supercomputers, ceramics, and biotechnology—the race is just beginning with the major tests of global market success yet to come. The established Japanese lead in volume production and sales of standardized memory chips may be an upscale example of the product cycle at work, for it is widely acknowledged that U.S. firms continue to hold leads in custom microprocessors and computer software. Further, the European two-engine Airbus and the Japanese RAM devices and IBM-compatible supercomputers exhibit market acumen as much as or more than technological prowess; these are all products that U.S. firms initially overlooked or at crucial points neglected to gear up to produce in sufficient quantity to meet demand. Nor should the supplier role of the United States be ignored as a source of exports and jobs; the Airbus incorporates a substantial amount of

U.S. technology, including its engines and some of its most sophisticated avionics.

Despite all of these caveats, the evidence is overwhelming of a widening technological parity and a quickness on the part of certain competitors to capitalize on newly acquired capabilities and seize important market niches at the high technology end of various high technology industries. Combined with the erosion of market share further down the technology scale, this adeptness places a premium on converting U.S. technological advantages into returns adequate to finance future research and development and investment in new ventures. Where they are not already, competitors soon will be poised to exploit almost any sign of weakness in this regard. The technological base will indeed become more specialized, not by abandoning major technological areas but by conceding markets for particular products in a number of fields. The danger is not that entire industries or leading producers will succumb to competition but that the process of innovation will be retarded.

Threats to U.S. Competitiveness

As in more mature sectors of the economy, the burden of adjusting to technological competition falls squarely on management and labor. Just as clearly, there are forces at work, beyond the firm's control, that are appropriate concerns of government. There has been no lack of attention to these forces. Rather, there is a need for analytical synthesis that can contribute to political consensus. A useful approach, therefore, is to identify the principal sources of U.S. vulnerabilities and to draw qualitative distinctions among these factors in a way that conveys a sense of their relative importance and, at the same time, has practical policy implications:

♦ Do the threats to U.S. competitiveness have broad, if uneven, impact on U.S. manufacturing and possibly other sectors or are the effects limited to particular industries or even specific technologies?

♦ Are the threats transitory or cyclical or do they represent long-term trends and structural changes?

♦ Do the threats raise issues for the domestic policy agenda primarily or must the United States try to persuade its trading partners to take unilateral or complementary actions to reduce them?

The following list is provisional, open-ended, and subject to revision in the light of new evidence. It is presented in rough order of priority with the caveat that many uncertainties and incommensurables make rankings a matter of judgment if not of guesswork.

General Threats

Exchange Rate Imbalance. The substantial (by various estimates, 20 to 25 percent) overvaluation of the dollar in exchange markets, in relation to underlying competitive relationships between the United States and its trading partners, poses an acute threat to both import-sensitive and export-oriented domestic industries in a wide range of sectors. The consequences are evident in the steadily worsening U.S. merchandise trade and current account deficits, which in 1984 totaled approximately $123 billion and $100 billion respectively. The Council of Economic Advisers has estimated that each 1 percent real dollar appreciation (adjusted for domestic price inflation) results roughly in a $2 billion increase in the trade deficit. This suggests that as much as one-half of the 1983 trade deficit was attributable to the dollar's rise since 1980.

Whether trade in high technology products in the aggregate is more or less exchange-rate sensitive than trade in other commodities and services is unclear and perhaps unanswerable. Some products are unique to the United States while others are standard and available from several sources. Technology-intensive U.S. industries export a far higher proportion (typically, 20 to 40 percent) of their domestic output than the average for manufacturing; but they also invest more heavily in foreign operations.

The effects of overvaluation are so pervasive that it is almost immaterial whether U.S. high technology trade is slightly more or less disadvantaged because of greater or lesser price elasticities and location of production. Along with other considerations, however, the intensity of U.S.-Japanese technological competition does compel particular attention to the yen-dollar imbalance.[5] By various calculations, an exchange rate of 180-200 Y/$ would be an "appropriate" equilibrium value, whereas the actual exchange rate, adjusted to 1982 prices, has fluctuated between 209 and 249 since 1980. The recent persistence of this misalignment should not obscure its spasmodic character, however. It occurred in the late 1960s and in the early to mid-1970s but disappeared in 1978 and 1979, when the yen briefly rose in value to the level of 170-190/dollar before falling precipitously.

Although a significant currency realignment can therefore be expected in the long term and is not inconceivable in a shorter time frame, it is obvious that so long as capital flows overwhelm trade flows in magnitude, the trade deficit will not by itself bring the dollar back in line, as once might have been the case. Furthermore, proponents of deliberate action, to stem both continued damage and protectionist reactions, agree that measures must be coordinated on a bilateral or even multilateral basis. It is not necessary to accept the frequent complaint of Japanese deliberate or indirect manipulation of the yen to conclude that the United States has neither the latitude in macroeconomic policy nor the leverage in international currency markets to bring about the needed exchange rate correction entirely on its own.

Relatively High Cost of Capital. The modest rise in capital spending, continuing even through the 1980-1982 recession, is commonly cited to dismiss suggestions that the United States has a chronic investment problem. Increasingly, however, the relevant comparisons are international rather than historical. By this standard, investment has been inadequate and too short term to meet the challenge posed by Japan. The share of the total GNP devoted to investment in manufacturing has fluctuated between 3 and 4 percent since the mid-1960s. By contrast, Japan undertook massive investment (7 to 9.5 percent of the GNP) during the late 1960s and early 1970s and continues to sustain a significantly higher rate than the United States.

Well-known differences in savings rates in part account for this disparity. Another major factor—and in all likelihood a more important determinant of international competitiveness than the narrowing U.S.-Japanese labor cost differential—is the relatively high cost of industrial capital in the United States. Recent estimates derived from different models indicate that the cost of capital to Japanese corporations is lower by a factor of at least two.[6] This differential has not affected the formation of start-up companies for which no comparable capital market exists in Japan; but it substantially raises the hurdle rate for long-term, high risk investments by established U.S. firms. By one calculation, a new venture requiring five years of development could justify only 40 percent as much private R&D investment in the United States as in Japan, assuming equal eventual returns. For a 10-year project, a Japanese company could invest five times as much in R&D.[7] Actual investment differentials are perhaps not of this magnitude but are nevertheless significant.

Despite the attention given high U.S. interest rates and foreign government subsidies, international capital cost differences are largely a function of corporate financial structures. By a ratio of 3 to 1, on average, U.S. firms rely heavily on equity financing even though its cost is almost 2.5 times that of debt, as a consequence of the risk premium on equity and the tax deductibility of interest on debt. The

58

pattern in Japan, and to a lesser extent in Europe, is the reverse; corporations are highly leveraged. Established Japanese firms have ready access to loans from banks that typically own large blocks of stock in those companies and are therefore willing to tolerate much higher debt burdens.

The U.S. capital cost disadvantage, having persisted since at least the early 1960s, increased dramatically in the late 1970s with the fall in stock prices and the rise in interest rates. Since then, the recovery in the value of corporate equities, decline in inflation, and reduction in corporate takes have combined to lower the overall cost of capital but by only a few percentage points—not nearly enough to narrow significantly the gap with Japan or lengthen substantially the time horizon for investment.

A related issue is the efficiency of capital allocation among industries and types of investments. Widely disparate U.S. tax rates on different assets and industries are well documented and recently have been contrasted with the more neutral Japanese corporate tax structure.[8] There is now evidence that, notwithstanding the temporary incremental R&D tax credit instituted in 1981, high technology industries experience higher average effective tax rates than U.S. manufacturing as a whole because their asset mix includes more intangibles like R&D taxed at a higher rate than those applying to structures and equipment.[9] If so, a neutral tax system that did not distort marketplace decisions would have accelerated the gradual investment shift that occurred in the 1970s from traditional manufacturing to high technology industries.

Corporate capital costs are also a reflection of nations' deeply imbedded decisions about the proper allocation of scarce capital between business investment and consumer consumption. Over all sectors, the cost of capital in the United States and Japan may be roughly equal. The United States maintains a much lower cost of capital in the housing sector, for example, by means of the many tax advantages attached to residential ownership; the same applies to consumer borrowing for purchases of durable goods such as automobiles. These priorities are negotiable only among domestic interest groups, not among nations. By the same token, they impose constraints on the ability of governments to reduce capital costs selectively.

Declining Quality of Education and Training. Depending upon the model, improved labor quality contributes 10 to 18 percent and technological innovation 44 to 72 percent to advances in productivity growth across the economy. Both are dependent in large part upon the skills of entry-level workers, the adaptability of the existing work force to changes in job requirements, and the supply of appropriately trained scientists and engineers. (The latter, which appears to be characterized by periodic shortages in particular specialties, is discussed below.)

By most accounts, including the judgment of several national study groups, the quality of precollege education in the United States has deteriorated relative to the system's performance of a decade or two ago. The decline is especially marked in science and mathematics education, not necessarily for the brightest students in the best schools who will eventually form the elite of professional scientists and engineers, but for the far larger number who will enter the work force as managers, technicians, and laborers without the science, math, and computer literacy increasingly required both in the factory and in the office. Nationwide, not merely here and there, curriculum requirements were relaxed, students elected fewer advanced science and math courses, test scores dropped, and teacher vacancies, driven up in part by expanding opportunities and better rewards in private industry, were filled with unqualified personnel.

The increasing mismatch between job requirements and labor skills is evidence that retraining opportunities have also declined, at least in relation to the pace of technological and structural economic change. Meanwhile, demographic changes place a premium on upgrading the skills of the present work force. After the explosive growth of employment in the 1970s, the rate of new entries is slowing down dramatically and the work force is aging. By 1990, workers who entered before 1983 will constitute 90 percent of the labor force; by the year 2000 the figure will still be 75 percent.

International comparisons of educational opportunities, requirements, and performance are of more doubtful validity than historical comparisons because of sharp cultural and organizational differences. The United States' extremely decentralized system does lead to more variation in practice and performance. The higher proportions of U.S. youths enrolled in secondary schools and universities do contribute to, as well as partially compensate for, deficiencies in quality. There do appear to be national differences in the degree to which creative thinking or rote learning is encouraged. Nevertheless, several indicators of curriculum quality and student achievement are adverse to the United States vis-à-vis both Japan and Western Europe.[10]

Specific Threats

Foreign Industrial Targeting. Governments have long maneuvered to establish, promote, and protect particular industries for reasons of

60

national security, as broadly conceived. The recently instituted state-orchestrated, industry-specific policies of many industrialized and developing countries, however, appear to be unprecedented in their frequency, the intensity, and concentration on the same group of industries, primarily those experiencing either rapid growth or adjustment to technological change and competition worldwide.

The United States is accustomed to, and has been moderately successful in dealing with, at-the-border trade barriers that were once the most visible techniques of industrial development and protection. Among the industrialized countries, tariffs and foreign investment restrictions have been gradually stripped away, exposing a range of practices—subtler forms of market protection, direct and indirect subsidies, credit allocation, and industrial reorganization and collaboration—that unquestionably influence trade but are defended by their practitioners as legitimate exercises of national sovereignty and essential contributors to their domestic growth and technological advancement.

Upon closer examination, the considerations that should govern the U.S. response to industrial targeting are complicated by many uncertainties apart from the absence of internationally agreed upon standards of conduct.

- ◆ The successes commonly attributed to national industrial policies may be the product of structural features of the economy reinforced by stable macroeconomic policies. Japanese consumer electronics and motorcycles and German chemicals and machinery have thrived without special government attention and encouragement.

- ◆ Some instruments of industrial policy—Japanese credit allocation for example—can be viewed as functional equivalents of private institutions—like equity markets—operating effectively in other market economies. Other forms of targeting such as direct support of R&D and tax system biases are less pervasive in Japan than in other industrialized countries including the United States.

- ◆ The use of targeting may achieve little more than creating a temporary foothold in internationally competitive industries. The French in computers, the Japanese in aluminum, and the British in commercial aircraft failed outright in their bids for enduring market positions, while in Japanese petrochemicals and German nuclear power government support has had to be redirected toward scaling back capacity created in the expectation of better markets or fewer low cost competitors.

♦ In such areas as semiconductors and machine tools, extensive Japanese government involvement in R&D and innovation has yet to yield technological breakthroughs propelling favored industries into world leadership.

♦ To the extent that industrial targeting contributes independently to competitiveness, it is hazardous to fix upon particular practices with a view to challenging or imitating them. The instruments employed vary considerably from industry to industry and over time. Any single instrument or set of instruments could turn out to be critical, marginal, irrelevant, or important but easily replaced by another technique serving the same purpose.

There are persuasive arguments against complacency while trying to determine the effects of industrial policies both in the targeting country and on its trading partners. Even skeptical analysts concede that selective government intervention can help to establish and maintain internationally competitive industries, provided that the support supplements market forces, preserves vigorous domestic competition, and builds upon a strong scientific and technological capability. Japanese authorities continue to intervene heavily in launching new high technology industries in spite of international and domestic pressures to reduce the government's role in industrial development. Presumably other countries with ambitious export objectives will try to duplicate measures perceived to be responsible for Japanese successes. And for U.S. producers, even temporary loss of major market share makes it difficult to maintain economies of scale that keep down production costs and help to finance successive rounds of innovation.

Restrictions on Foreign Market Access. The fact that no significant high technology market can be taken any longer for granted or considered dispensable makes for a long list of trade concerns. The more intractable budget deficits and exchange rates appear, at least in the short term, the more attention focuses on government-imposed or sanctioned impediments to U.S. exports and investment. These diverse measures vary by industry and product as well as by region and country. The list encompasses all of the conventional barriers—tariffs, quotas, and investment performance requirements—together with the following practices that have a particularly important bearing on trade in technology-intensive goods and related services:

♦ tightly controlled access to purchasing by governments and state-run enterprises, notably telecommunications monopolies;

♦ disregard of corporate intellectual property rights, including compulsory disclosure of proprietary data or licensing of technology;

♦ discriminatory application of product technical and safety standards and testing requirements; and

♦ subsidies to domestic research, development, and innovation.

Very roughly, these obstacles sort themselves out as industrial or developing country issues, simply by virtue of differences in economic development and degrees of integration into the international trading system and adherence to its codes of conduct. Vis-à-vis Europe and Japan, procurement, subsidies, and standards are more troublesome, while in developing country markets, traditional trade barriers and performance requirements represent the greater burden.

It is no accident that complaints against and negotiations with the Japanese have received the most emphasis. As the world's second largest market, Japan theoretically presents unparalleled export opportunities for U.S. businesses. A strong U.S. presence in the Japanese market would facilitate access to that country's rapid advances in product and process technology and strengthen the U.S. competitive position in third country markets. According to statistical trends in bilateral trade, however, the United States is losing rather than gaining market share in such products as semiconductors, computers, and telecommunications equipment. Japan has the lowest level of foreign direct investment of any major industrialized country.

The fact that the United States is not doing especially well is not necessarily evidence that the Japanese are behaving badly, at least to the extent of maintaining a "fundamentally closed" market. Contrary to the conventional wisdom, there may be nothing grossly abnormal about Japan's admittedly unique trade structure (exceedingly low imports of manufactured goods), when allowance is made for international differences in resource endowments, labor and capital quality and quantity, distance from trading partners, and other factors that determine comparative advantage.[11] In essence, Japan is compelled to run a large trade surplus in manufactured goods to pay for its imports of raw materials and services.

Historically insular and protectionist, Japan reversed course in the 1970s by adopting a series of trade liberalization policies under intense domestic and international pressures. It cut tariffs on average below levels prevailing in the United States and Europe; limited quotas primarily to agricultural commodities; relaxed controls on internal capital markets and foreign investment; and more recently concluded agreements on product standards and safety testing, public procurement, domestic and export subsidies, and access to government-sponsored research and development projects and their proprietary results. At best, additional formal liberalization measures promise marginal improvement in the overall U.S. trade balance with Japan.

For particular U.S. industries, however, a series of subtle constraints can add up to major impediments to U.S. exports and investments in a critical market. In electronics and telecommunications, for example, the constraints probably include uncertain protection of semiconductor designs and software programs, the "buy national" proclivity of the public telecommunications monopoly Nipon Telegraph and Telephone Public Corporation (NTT) and protection of the infant Japanese communications satellite industry.

Progress continues to be made on some sectoral issues through bilateral discussions, but other subjects of vigorous complaint relate to aspects of industrial and financial structure that do not lend themselves readily to negotiation. The harmonization of Japanese economic institutions with prevailing international practice will continue to be a slow, incremental process driven as much by internal change as by external demands.

Technical Resource Deficiencies. There is no convincing evidence that overall R&D spending patterns among the industrialized countries account either for the U.S. slippage or the rapid advances made by Japan and other competitors. U.S. R&D funding did remain constant from the mid-1960s through the early 1970s as other nations increased their expenditures in real terms and as a proportion of economic output; but the lack of real growth in the United States was primarily the result of cutbacks in government funding of defense and space-related projects with at best indirect commercial applications. Since the mid-1970s, U.S. expenditures have resumed real growth at a rate comparable to those of Japan, Germany, and France. The recovery stems largely from steady growth in private sector spending combined with a resumption of modest growth in federal government funding. During the last decade, the United States spent as much for research and development as its 12 leading industrial trading partners combined.[12]

Aggregate figures, of course, obscure questions of allocation. It is some concern that during the last decade private industry resources were shifted from long-term research to short-term applied research and product development promising more immediate financial returns but fewer major innovations. This trend is probably best viewed, however, as a function of macroeconomic conditions, not as a by-product of R&D-related public policies.

Particular R&D deficiencies and opportunities have received less public attention than the rapid productivity gains and technological advances of foreign competitors probably warrant. Some of these

64

deficiencies appear to lie in process-related fields where the benefits of technological improvements accrue to many companies or several related industries but are not easily captured by the innovator. It seems likely that the United States has underinvested relative to Japan in long-range applied research relating to a wide range of manufacturing technologies including metal-working machine tools, flexible manufacturing systems, and biological process engineering. Other deficiencies may derive from the inability of all but the largest firms in highly competitive industries such as semiconductors and computers to finance independently the skyrocketing costs of new generation product development.

U.S. industry possesses the largest concentration of highly trained, highly mobile scientists and engineers, but in the last decade shortages developed in critical specialities—primarily in computer science and electrical engineering but reportedly also in industrial engineering, solid-state and plasma physics, optics, and polymer chemistry. As the electronics industry tripled in size during the 1970s, the number of electrical engineering graduates remained constant. Japan's rate of production of engineers of all specialities greatly exceeds that of the United States.[13]

Undergraduate engineering enrollments have expanded in response to demand, but the education market is an imperfect one. An estimated 10 percent of junior engineering faculty positions are vacant, 25 percent in computer science and electronics, as business woos and wins graduates with more than competitive salaries. There has been a drop in the number of engineering doctoral candidates, threatening to exacerbate the shortage of faculty given prospective retirement rates. Meanwhile, the rapid obsolescence of university research facilities and equipment endangers the heretofore undisputed quality of U.S. higher education in the sciences and engineering. An estimated backlog of $1 billion to $4 billion has accumulated, partly as a result of cutbacks in federal budgets for university construction and instrumentation. The difficulty in these circumstances of replacing, let alone expanding, faculty and laboratories has led some institutions to contravene demand and supply by capping undergraduate engineering admissions.

Policy Directions

The United States no longer has a commanding edge in the development and commercialization of all major industrial technologies. The emergence of a multipolar global economy is accompanied by a protracted struggle for economic position and advantage. The U.S.-

Japanese rivalry is the immediate locus of tension, but that will shift from time to time and depending upon which industries are regarded as having strategic national importance. In this new era of technological competition, the United States has enduring interests in preserving its comparative advantage in a diversity of sectors, in defending the Western alliance against fragmentation born of economic rivalry, and in maintaining a relatively open trading system in which international commerce will continue to fuel economic development.

These objectives are not easily served, let alone reconciled, in a context where the scope for effective government action is limited by the bluntness of its instruments and the internationalization of economic activity. In a market economy, after all, the management of technology is predominantly in private rather than in government hands. Public instruments of fiscal and monetary policy, investment in research and development and technical manpower training, protection of intellectual property, procurement, and trade promotion and regulation have multiple effects that are primarily indirect, sometimes marginal, and usually difficult to predict with assurance. U.S. and foreign companies, moreover, are engaging in technology exchanges and joint ventures on an unprecedented scale to circumvent trade barriers, lower costs, comply with foreign investment restrictions, and simply acquire superior equipment and know-how. These trends militate against national governments' attempts at exclusive control of technologies, whether for economic or security purposes.

Be that as it may, the previous analysis suggests a domestic policy agenda for the United States, encompassing macroeconomic policies and measures affecting the cost of capital and the adequacy of technical resources, and an international agenda, including issues of foreign government economic policy, market access, and generally the terms and rules of trade. The distinction between general and specific competitive threats forces consideration of linkages between high technology industries and other sectors of the economy as well as the advisability of expanding sector-specific interventions. The distinction between cyclical and long-term problems highlights the necessity of compromises between short-run and long-range objectives and between these and political realities.

Domestic Policy Agenda

Macroeconomic Policy. The mix of monetary and fiscal policies, as other essays in this volume attest, is at once responsible for much of the adjustment burden being borne by U.S. manufacturing and yet is

66

the only suitable means of correcting the economy's erratic growth pattern and its inordinately strong currency. In particular, exchange rate realignment, to the extent that it is manipulable, must be managed carefully in light of the partially compensating benefits of an overvalued dollar—an influx of foreign investment capital and cheap goods helping to restrain interest rates and inflation while sustaining investment. Intervention in currency markets is ineffective except as a marginal, short-term expedient; and capital controls risk a resumption of interest rate hikes and price increases. Only adjustments in macroeconomic policy can accomplish the unavoidable trade-offs with acceptable results.

There is broad agreement that the current mix of fiscal and monetary policies should be altered by reducing the long-run federal budget deficit and thereby allowing the Federal Reserve to adopt a steadier expansionary stance. This shift would improve the competitiveness of all U.S. firms engaged in international trade by weakening the dollar, lowering real interest rates, and stimulating demand and investment.[14]

Lowering Capital Costs. The availability and cost of capital in Japan are primarily functions of an exceedingly high personal savings rate and close affiliations of banks with large corporations. It may be necessary for the United States to adopt additional incentives to savings, at the expense of consumption, to generate the capital required for technology-intensive industries to remain competitive and for more mature industries to modernize; but it is neither feasible nor perhaps wise to encourage extensive bank participation in equity ownership to promote greater corporate reliance on debt financing. The latter would require a radical overhaul of U.S. banking regulation and conflict with a tradition of separation between industrial organizations and financial institutions. In any case, the long-term equity holdings that give Japanese banks a proprietary interest in lending to affiliated corporations would be an anomaly in the much more fluid U.S. stock market.

Changes in the tax code are therefore the preferred vehicle for lowering the cost of investment capital in the United States. Several alternatives have been proposed, including cutting the corporate tax rate or eliminating the corporate tax altogether; permitting stock dividend payments to be deducted or otherwise reclassifying equity as debt; allowing immediate expensing of new investment in plant, equipment, inventory, and research and development; and liberalizing and extending the R&D tax credit.

Such measures, necessarily, fly directly in the face of the imperative to reduce the fiscal deficit. They are at odds, too, with a redistribution of the individual and corporate tax burdens proposed in the name of tax reform. The conjunction of the reform movement with pressures for revenue increases nevertheless expands the range of options that will be considered and underscores the need for long-range criteria in evaluating them.

♦ Care should be taken to avoid discouraging new investment by raising significantly the cost of financial capital in relation to competitors' costs. This implies that the burden of any tax increase should fall primarily on consumption or on returns to previous investment.

♦ The strong arguments for reducing distortions in the corporate tax structure's treatment of different assets and industries should be heeded. A more neutral tax system with incentives for new investment would facilitate the movement of capital from declining to growth sectors without denying basic industries the capital desperately needed for modernization, including purchasing of high technology capital goods.

♦ It is important to preserve the vitality of the venture capital market, an asset unique to the United States and the envy of many industrial countries. This cannot be taken for granted. In the mid-1970s only a handful of entrepreneurs managed to obtain financing to launch new companies; in 1982 venture capital firms invested nearly $750 million in young enterprises. The turnaround is attributed largely to the capital gains tax reductions of 1978 and 1981.

Improving Human and Technical Resources. Upgrading primary and secondary education, increasing worker retraining opportunities, overcoming shortages of teachers and graduates, updating university facilities and equipment, and directing additional resources to certain areas of research and development require a variety of concerted and independent efforts on the part of governments at all levels, universities, labor organizations, and industry. Recent actions and proposals that merit consideration include

♦ differential and merit pay for public school teachers and university faculty in demand by industry,

♦ forgivable education loans for prospective science and math instructors and engineering students committing themselves to teaching careers,

♦ expanded use of industrial engineers and scientists as adjunct university faculty,

♦ strengthening of science and math requirements for secondary school and college graduation,

- increased incentives or direct funding for university construction and acquisition of state-of-the-art research equipment,
- increased tax credits for business investment in worker education and training,
- creation of an Individual Training Account comparable to the Individual Retirement Account (IRA),
- educational vouchers financed by a new component of the unemployment insurance system,
- an explicit exemption from antitrust liability for cooperative ventures aimed at basic research and generic technology development, and
- increased use of limited R&D partnerships to fund high risk research.

In these diverse areas (with the exceptions of university, defense, and space research), the federal government has a circumscribed if important role as a direct provider of financial support and services. It should and, of fiscal necessity, probably must continue to be the government's principal role to stimulate initiative and experimentation rather than to undertake large-scale programs unless its own requirements justify them.

Recent developments in applied microelectronic and computer research illustrate these propositions. The Pentagon has launched ambitious product development efforts in high-speed integrated circuits (VHSIC) and so-called fifth-generation computers. No doubt prompted in part by civilian Japanese programs in related areas, these projects may have important commercial spin-offs; but they are directed at specific military needs with few immediate civilian counterparts. Independently and in direct response to the Japanese commercial challenge, firms in the semiconductor and computer industries are collaborating on equally ambitious but more basic research objectives. These receive Defense Department (DOD) funds in areas of technology relevant to the military's programs. More important, they have been given a separate boost by legislation limiting their antitrust exposure.

A strong theoretical case can be made for non-DOD public funding of civilian generic technology (as distinct from proprietary product) development. Legislation is in place authorizing the Department of Commerce to sponsor centers of such activity jointly with industry. Nevertheless, the history of comparable undertakings in energy, transportation, and housing is not encouraging. Success in these efforts is unlikely without private sector initiative and guidance.[15] For the time being, extremely limited federal resources would best be concentrated on shoring up the civilian science and engineering base.

Selective Industrial Policies? The case simply has not been made for providing direct low-cost financing or subsidizing or guaranteeing credit on concessionary terms to selected growth industries and firms. The need for cheaper capital is not confined to the high technology sector whose growth, in any case, is linked to productivity improvements and product innovations in basic industries. Moreover, the United States, in contrast to Japan and most European countries, lacks a tradition and accepted mechanisms for discriminating among competing enterprises on the basis of commercial performance and prospects for success in international trade. The precedents frequently cited are inappropriate. In defense and space program procurement, source selections are either highly regulated to ensure competition or are based on a contractor's unique capacity to meet an overriding national need. In agriculture, producers historically have not considered themselves in direct competition with one another and therefore have not been threatened by the government's extensive involvement in R&D, production, and marketing.

A tax-based industrial policy providing additional incentives to research, replacement of capital stock, acquisition of foreign technology, and other innovation-related investments would not raise objections that some firms were directly benefiting at the expense of their closest rivals. The approach would have considerable merit were it not for the likelihood that it would encourage demands for other special purpose tax provisions, compounding distortions in the tax structure, not necessarily to the benefit of high technology industries. The United States presently has a tax-based industrial policy reflecting no particular economic rationale but rather the relative political influence of various constituencies.

International Trade Agenda

How the United States organizes its economic affairs to respond to the competitive challenge in high technology has a direct bearing on how it approaches and what it can reasonably demand of its trading partners. The processes, begun only recently, of sorting out domestic and international objectives must go hand in hand. These are far from simple tasks. If there is uncertainty about the priority of domestic initiatives and in some cases reluctance to bear their costs, the trade policy debate exhibits sharp disagreement over U.S. purposes and negotiating strategy. These differences greatly complicate dealings with other producers, particularly the Japanese, who, regardless of their flexibility or inflexibility on issues in dispute, understandably may be confused about U.S. intentions.

Pressures are mounting to invoke aggressive trade measures to halt the deterioration in the overall and high technology trade balances. As a rule, however, trade instruments cannot reverse worldwide or bilateral deficits of the magnitude the United States is experiencing as a consequence mainly of cyclical and structural economic factors. Overreliance on import curbs and export incentives exacerbates public frustration as long as the underlying causes of adverse trade trends are not addressed. All too often in these circumstances, the recourse is to more extensive micro-management of trade flows rather than a search for alternative—for example, macroeconomic policy—solutions.

The appropriate goals of trade policy under present law are both narrower and longer term:

- to reduce or remove particular bilateral trade impediments,
- to curb unfair foreign trading practices such as dumping and certain forms of subsidies,
- to enable U.S. producers to compete on roughly comparable terms in financing foreign sales,
- to provide domestic industries a temporary respite from fair but injurious import competition, and
- to arrive at mutually agreed upon terms of trade and rules of conduct that approximate the ideal of a liberal global trading system.

Government actions in several of these categories are prompted by private sector initiatives and therefore reflect narrow interests rather than objective economic criteria. Invariably, progress is incremental. This explains why trade actions and agreements can rarely be expected to bring about major improvements in year-to-year trade balances or other short-term macroeconomic indices. Nevertheless, it does not diminish their potential importance in the near term to particular industries and firms or to the economy's performance in the long run. A case in point is the recent relaxation of Japanese government controls on internal capital markets, in part in response to pressures exerted by the United States. Despite their failure to give an immediate boost to the value of the yen, the steps being taken by Japan promise over a longer period to facilitate a realignment in the exchange rate as well as increases in foreign investment and, indirectly, U.S. exports.[16]

Agreement on realistic trade policy objectives would not by itself resolve the concurrent debate over negotiating strategy. One constituency adheres to the traditional approach of first working out multi-lateral rules regulating government interventions in such forums as GATT. Should a competitor's practices pose a "specific" threat, the United States may be obliged to initiate bilateral discussions, although again these should be conducted "within the framework of GATT and other appropriate multilateral institutions." Only in the event that discussions fail and damage is "imminent" should the United States resort to unilateral actions to protect its interests.[17] Others would reverse this sequence by having the United States first demonstrate its resolve to curb foreign government interventions through unilateral actions under strengthened and streamlined trade laws before engaging in either bilateral or multilateral negotiations. This view considers both U.S. bargaining leverage and international institutions too weak at present to serve U.S. interests.[18]

In practice, the United States is pursuing all three options simultaneously. Because the president has urged an early start to a new round of multilateral trade negotiations, bilateral discussions with the Japanese and others are entering a new phase, and because unilateral actions are being pressed upon and by the Reagan administration, there is some urgency attached to reviewing the aims and instruments of U.S. trade policy as they bear on high technology industries.

Multilateral Negotiations. New international rules governing national industrial targeting, barriers to services and investment, and related issues are a distant prospect. Major U.S. trading partners have dragged their feet in endorsing a new GATT round, let alone in acceding to a specific agenda. Some signatories, such as Brazil, that would be most affected by such negotiations remain under tremendous pressure to enhance their export potential while maintaining a relatively protected home market. And as yet there is no domestic political consensus on U.S. objectives.

Realism, however, should not deter domestic and international preparations for multilateral discussions not exclusively under GATT but, where appropriate, in other forums. The most urgent task is a clarification of U.S. interests and setting of priorities on the basis not only of economic stakes but also prospects for agreement. Along with reducing barriers to services trade, clarifying safeguard procedures, and streamlining the GATT dispute settlement process, leading candidates for negotiation include harmonizing domestic subsidy practices, securing more uniform protection of conventional and novel forms of intellectual property, and narrowing the scope of public procurement restrictions and investment performance requirements.

Each of these issues will be exceedingly difficult to resolve because many nations, not least the United States, consider their current practices as basic elements of industrial development or national security policy. The U.S. military represents the world's largest protected market for high technology goods, and U.S. support of defense-related R&D dwarfs other governments' investments. Prevailing international rules, including the new GATT subsidy and procurement codes, are therefore quite permissive. Modest progress is not inconceivable, however, if the direct and indirect costs of unrestrained subsidization and protection can be plausibly demonstrated and objectionable practices can be defined with some precision. It may be possible, for example, to reach agreements limiting civilian R&D support to generic technology research as distinct from commercial product development and enabling foreign-owned domestic corporations to participate in government-sponsored R&D projects on a reciprocal basis.[19]

Bilateral Negotiations. Certain trade issues cannot or need not be deferred for the several years required to conclude even a piecemeal GATT round. In these cases bilateral and even sector-specific discussions hold some promise for clarifying and ameliorating differences with major trading partners before the stakes become so high that they evolve into major disputes. U.S. negotiators have had some success in persuading the Japanese to liberalize capital markets, open NTT procurement to U.S. suppliers, allow U.S. subsidiaries access to government-sponsored R&D results, accept U.S. product testing results, and at least temporarily shelve plans for discriminatory legislation in telecommunications and electronics. Although this approach entails some risk of dividing trade into mini-systems separated by highly specialized and exclusive arrangements, it also provides an opportunity to establish models for eventual multilateral agreements.

An appropriate test of bilateral trade deals in high technology is their consistency with long-range U.S. interests in expanding market access and reducing government intervention. The corresponding danger is the use of bilateralism to parcel out shares of existing markets. The negotiated export restraints now proliferating in steel and permanently entrenched in textiles do not represent an attractive or even practical method of dealing with competitive problems in industries characterized by rapid innovation and relatively short product life cycles. Forcing the Japanese to establish quantitative targets for high technology imports would be equally problematic. In either case quotas are product-specific or they are largely meaningless. The allocation of Japanese production or import consumption must be negotiated and monitored if not centrally determined. There are inevitable pressures to include third country suppliers to the United States or Japan in such arrangements. The perverse result is to reinforce and very likely expand governments' involvement in their domestic economies. A far better response to outcries over the mounting bilateral trade deficit is to press the Japanese to pursue a more expansionist macroeconomic policy course along with further market liberalization.

Unilateral Actions. For high technology industries especially, import relief, other than in cases of foreign dumping or other patently unfair trade practices, is an instrument of limited utility and is invoked at some risk. The mere prospect of a concerted foreign technological development effort may deter U.S. investment needed to sustain innovation. The practice that is the object of a complaint may not be a principal source of the competitive threat or may have been suspended by the time exporting to the United States begins in volume. Deterrence may only be effective before the threat fully materializes. Relief, when granted, may have been overtaken by the pace of innovation. The offending country may retaliate against unrelated U.S. products and investments. By maintaining the United States' traditional reliance on privately initiated trade complaints showing evidence of material or imminent injury, recent amendments to the standard trade remedy laws deal only marginally with these possibilities or not at all.

The Trade and Tariff Act of 1984 has nevertheless strengthened to some extent section 301 of the Trade Act of 1974, a rarely invoked but uniquely designed instrument to enforce U.S. access to foreign markets. The president and the U.S. trade representative have broad discretion under section 301 to initiate actions while trade-distorting foreign government practices are in place but before injury to U.S. firms has occurred. Retaliation may take the form of curtailing previous trade concessions, imposing import duties, otherwise restricting imports, or, conceivably, providing countervailing domestic subsidies. It may be directed at a targeted product or at a more immediately vulnerable product or service of the offending country.[20]

Such unilateral actions are obviously not to be undertaken lightly or routinely as they risk foreign retaliation and possibly challenge in GATT. Primarily as a negotiating tactic to overcome competitors' resistance to accommodation, however, a carefully timed and targeted section 301 action deserves consideration. It could signal the United States' determination to prevent the systematic undermining of its key competitive advantages.

Notes

1. Trade balances in two other major surplus categories— services and agricultural products—are to a greater degree governed by

74

unpredictable factors such as the flow of investment capital into and out of the United States, political relations with nonmarket countries, and weather conditions.

2. See Paula Stern, "The Drawbacks of Traditional U.S. Trade Strategies," in Stephen Merrill, ed., *U.S. Strategies and Foreign Industrial Targeting: A Report of a CSIS Conference* (Washington, D.C.: Center for Strategic and International Studies, 1983), 17-22.

3. U.S. Department of Commerce International Trade Administration, *An Assessment of U.S. Competitiveness in High Technology Industries* (Washington, D.C.: 1983), 3-4.

4. In another analysis of U.S. high technology trade performance, 7 of 10 industry groups were found to have lost market share between 1970 and 1980, with agricultural chemicals making the only significant gain. Bruce R. Scott, "National Strategy for Stronger U.S. Competitiveness," *Harvard Business Review*, March-April (1984), 82. These findings are not at odds with the evidence that high technology industries outperformed low technology manufacturing and thus increased their comparative advantage. Similarly, loss of high technology market share is consistent with the bullish judgment of several economists that U.S. manufacturing as a whole neither suffered a major loss of competitiveness nor exhibited a pattern of "deindustrialization" during the last decade. See *U.S. Industrial Competitiveness: Perception and Reality* (New York: New York Stock Exchange, 1984), 18, that puts the ratio of U.S. high technology industry market share losers to gainers at 8 to 4.

5. See C. Fred Bergsten, "U.S. Economic Relations with Japan: The Impact of the Yen-Dollar Exchange Rate," testimony before the Senate Foreign Relations Committee (April 7, 1983).

6. George N. Hatsopoulos, *High Cost of Capital: Handicap of U.S. Industry* (American Business Conference, Inc., and Thermo Electron Corporation: 1983); U.S. Department of Commerce International Trade Administration, *A Historical Comparison of the Cost of Financial Capital in France, the Federal Republic of Germany, Japan, and the United States* (Washington: 1983). These studies were critically reviewed at a CSIS conference on July 25, 1983. A summary of the discussion is available.

7. Hatsopoulos, *High Cost of Capital*, Executive Summary, 9.

8. See Mervyn King and Don Fullerton, eds., *Taxation of Income from Capital: A Comparative Study of the U.S., U.K., Sweden and West Germany* (Chicago: University of Chicago Press, 1984).

9. Charles R. Hulten and James W. Robertson, "The Taxation of High Technology Industries," *National Tax Journal*, vol. 37, no. 3 (September 1984), 327-345.

10. See Joseph Mintzes, "Scientific and Technical Personnel Trends and Competitiveness of U.S. Technologically Intensive and Critical Industries," paper prepared for the Division of Policy Research and Analysis, National Science Foundation (1982).

11. Gary R. Saxonhouse, "The Micro- and Macroeconomics of Foreign Sales to Japan," in William Cline, ed., *Trade Policy in the 1980s* (Washington, D.C.: Institute for International Economics, 1983), 272-275.

12. Rolf Peikarz, Eleanor Thomas, and Donna Jennings, "International Comparisons of Research and Development Expenditures," paper prepared by the Division of Policy Research and Analysis, National Science Foundation (January 1983).

13. The Business-Higher Education Forum, *Engineering Manpower and Education: Foundation for Future Competitiveness* (Washington, D.C.: October 1982).

14. Robert Z. Lawrence, *Can America Compete?* (Washington, D.C.: The Brookings Institution, 1984), 10.

15. Richard R. Nelson, "Policies in Support of High Technology Industries," working paper of the Institution for Social and Policy Studies (New Haven, Conn.: Yale University, April 1984), 121-124.

16. Saxonhouse, "The Micro- and Macroeconomics of Foreign Sales to Japan," 283-285.

17. *International Competition in Advanced Technology: Decisions for America*, Report of the National Research Council Panel on Advanced Technology Competition and the Industrialized Allies (Washington, D.C.: National Academy Press, 1983), 8-10.

18. The Labor-Industry Coalition for International Trade, *International Trade, Industrial Policies, and the Future of American Industry* (Washington, D.C.: 1983), 65-66.

19. Gary Clyde Hufbauer and Joanna Shelton Erb, *Subsidies in International Trade* (Washington, D.C.: Institute for International Economics, 1984), 103-104, 107-110.

20. U.S. International Trade Commission, *Foreign Industrial Targeting and its Effects on U.S. Industries, Phase I: Japan* (Washington, D.C.: 1983), 42-45.

Business Cycles, Macroeconomic Policy, and U.S. Industrial Performance

by
Gordon Richards

In recent years there has been an emerging debate as to the relative roles of cyclical and structural factors in the performance of the U.S. economy over the last two decades. In structural interpretations, the economy is theorized to have undergone a series of adverse longer-term changes, producing a secular deterioration in industrial performance during the 1970s. Some versions of this thesis call for various forms of industrial or structural adjustment policy to reverse this deterioration. Conversely, in cyclical interpretations, the central role of business cycles implies that the determinants of economic performance have been concerned primarily with macroeconomic policy. The implication is that the appropriate policy instruments for bringing the economy back to its long-term growth trajectory are not industrial policies aimed at structural adjustment but traditional stabilization tools.

To some extent, the preferability of cyclical or structural interpretations depends on the choice of the dependent variable. Cyclical interpretations have tended to emphasize movements in total economic activity and have modeled developments in individual sectors primarily as a function of variations in the GNP and aggregate demand. Structural interpretations, on the other hand, have emphasized factors such as changes in the output mix, a secular decline in productivity growth and international competitiveness, decreases in capital inputs, slower gains in R&D spending, and a deterioration in the quality of microeconomic decision making. Both cyclical and structural interpretations have acknowledged some role for exogenous disturbances. The energy shocks caused by the increases in OPEC oil prices had a pronounced impact on the economy, both because they led to restrictive monetary policies that threw the economy into recession and because changes in relative factor prices had adverse effects on the productive structure. A second disturbance to the economy had to do with the massive growth in the labor force during the 1970s. The resulting increase in the natural rate of unemployment appears to have contributed to the destabilizing course of macroeconomic policy.

This paper is primarily concerned with macroeconomic policy and the business cycle, and the analysis is at the aggregate rather than the sectoral level. Although structural arguments are subordinated, this does not imply that secular forces were entirely absent or did not account for some aspects of economic performance. Nevertheless, structural factors are dealt with here insofar as they influenced macroeconomic policy and, indirectly, cyclical swings.

The basic thesis is that increased cyclical volatility in the 1970s and early 1980s is attributable to destabilizing macroeconomic policies. Structural factors such as the OPEC shocks and the explosion in the labor force were partially responsible, however, for the conduct of demand management. The greater magnitude of recessions since the mid-1970s resulted from the combination of the OPEC shocks and the restrictive reaction of macroeconomic policy. The booms of the early and the late 1970s were achieved through the prolongation of reflationary policies until the latter stages of recoveries and these policies were in part an effort to achieve full employment in the face of unprecedented growth in the labor force. The result was that demand management exhibited a procyclical bias that exacerbated cyclical movements in output and inflation.

Although structural factors help explain business cycles, they do not provide a complete picture. Macroeconomic policy did not merely respond to oil price increases and labor force growth but was dictated independently by political factors. An understanding of the economy's performance during the 1970s therefore requires not merely an acknowledgement of policy responses to exogenous disturbances but also an explanation of political determinants of macroeconomic decision making.

The major portion of this paper reviews in some detail cyclical developments during the 1970s. First, however, is an examination of the cyclical versus structural debate. The final section examines the causes of macroeconomic instability and provides some preliminary policy recommendations.

Cyclical versus Structural Interpretations

The decision to emphasize macroeconomic policy and the business cycle as determinants of economic performance cannot be made a priori. Instead, a review of major developments in the economy during the 1970s is necessary at the outset to assess the relative strengths and weaknesses of cyclical and structural interpretations. The indicators surveyed here include benchmark measures of aggregate economic activity—industrial production and capital investment—along with productivity, R&D spending, international trade, and employment. Even where there is evidence of a role for structural factors, cyclical variations explain a significant component of the behavior of these indicators. To be sure, there is an unambiguous role for structural factors such as the increase in relative energy prices and the demographic explosion in the work force during the 1970s. But these developments are of interest at least as much for their influence on macroeconomic policy as for their independent effects on the productive structure. In this sense, they can be viewed as indirect determinants of the business cycle.

Industrial Growth and Investment

In comparing the aggregate performance of the economy during the 1970s to the previous decade, there is no evidence of structural decline in real GNP growth or industrial production. Instead, what is particularly striking about the period from the 1970s onward is that slower average growth was attributable largely to the greater depth and frequency of the downturns in the business cycle. Table 1 gives the annual growth rates of real GNP, industrial production, and manufacturing output for the period 1962 to 1983. During the 1960s, the economy underwent approximately eight years of continuous growth, interrupted by only one minor slowdown in 1967. Beyond this point, however, there is evidence of considerably greater business cycle volatility. During the periods of expansion, the growth rates of real GNP, industrial production, and manufacturing output all achieved levels comparable to or greater than those experienced during the 1960s. There is, therefore, no basis for positing a secular decline in manufacturing or long-term "deindustrialization." Instead, the lower average growth rate from the 1970s onward reflects the severe contractions in output during the major recessionary periods, 1974 to 1975 and 1980 to 1982.

Further evidence supporting a cyclical interpretation of industrial performance is provided in econometric tests by Robert Lawrence (1984). When the index of industrial production is regressed on the GNP, not only is a very high percentage of the variance explained, but the equation closely replicates the actual behavior of industrial output during the 1970s. In other words, the growth rate of industrial pro-

TABLE 1

Domestic Economic Indicators, 1962–1983 (Annual Percent Change)

Year	Gross National Product	Industrial Production	Manufacturing Production	Gross Domestic Private Investment	Net Domestic Private Investment	Productivity Growth*	R&D Spending
1962	5.8%	8.25%	8.99%	13.19%	30.33%	3.6%	5.8%
1963	4.0	5.96	6.01	6.46	10.45	3.2	8.7
1964	5.3	6.80	6.86	6.31	9.64	3.9	9.2
1965	6.0	9.91	9.51	14.21	25.73	3.1	3.8
1966	6.0	8.91	9.14	7.31	9.20	2.5	5.5
1967	2.7	2.25	2.15	−4.97	−14.35	1.9	2.8
1968	4.6	6.30	6.40	4.33	3.33	3.3	2.0
1969	2.8	4.52	4.32	6.06	7.11	−0.3	0.6
1970	−0.2	−2.97	−4.14	−7.53	−21.80	0.3	−3.7
1971	3.4	1.67	1.69	9.72	17.95	3.3	−2.4
1972	5.7	9.22	9.89	12.13	20.38	3.7	2.1
1973	5.8	8.44	9.17	11.54	20.54	2.4	2.4
1974	−0.6	−0.39	−0.31	−10.11	−25.75	−2.5	−1.0
1975	−1.2	−8.89	−10.12	−20.82	−57.12	2.0	2.0
1976	5.4	10.78	12.04	19.19	74.71	3.2	4.6
1977	5.5	5.90	6.22	10.68	14.91	2.2	4.0
1978	5.0	5.72	6.07	10.04	19.69	0.6	4.2
1979	2.8	4.38	4.63	−0.17	−7.53	−1.5	5.3
1980	−0.3	−3.61	−4.49	−11.76	−37.08	−0.7	4.1
1981	2.6	2.72	2.52	9.16	21.98	1.9	2.8**
1982	−1.9	−8.21	−8.51	−14.54	−55.31	−0.1	2.2**
1983	3.3	6.57	7.92	12.29	50.94	3.1	N/A

* Nonfarm Business Sector
** Preliminary Estimates
Source: National Science Foundation, Department of Commerce, Federal Reserve.

duction is explained largely by aggregate economic activity, and there is no evidence of a decline in manufacturing relative to total GNP.[1]

Essentially the same pattern applies to capital formation. Table 1 provides data on gross and net domestic private investment for the period 1962 to 1983. As with industrial production, capital investment shows much greater evidence of cyclical volatility than of secular stagnation. During the recoveries of the 1970s, the growth rates of both gross and net domestic investment averaged above those of the 1960s. The acceleration in the growth rate of net fixed investment during the late 1970s is particularly marked. The speed of expansion of investment during the recovery periods, however, was at least partially as compensatory—a response in some sense to contractions in investment produced by downturns in the business cycle in conjunction with the energy shocks and increases in the user cost of capital. What occurred in the capital sector was an increase in the magnitude of business cycle fluctuations; the depth of the recessionary downturn tends to explain the strength of the ensuing rebounds. Year-to-year movements in capital spending were more jagged than in previous periods, particularly the 1960s; but no structural decline was in evidence.

Productivity

Although the performance of industrial production and capital investment appears to have been dominated by cyclical rather than structural factors, in certain other areas, notably productivity, there is evidence that adverse secular forces also were at work during the 1970s. Since the mid-1970s, a marked deterioration in the rate of productivity growth occurred in the United States and throughout the industrial countries. Productivity growth rates initially slackened in late 1973 and declined sharply in 1974. Thereafter, productivity growth underwent a cyclical recovery in 1975-1978, although it did not attain the growth rates experienced during previous expansionary periods. In the United States, productivity growth was well below trend during the later stages of the 1975-1979 recovery. Beginning in 1979, productivity growth again became negative. A normal cyclical recovery in productivity growth, comparable to the earlier recovery in 1976, occurred in 1982, however.

The causes of the productivity decline have been examined in numerous econometric studies.[2] The contribution of cyclical factors is readily apparent. Productivity initially underwent a mild slowdown during the late 1960s, notwithstanding continuous economic expansion, in part because of high rates of labor utilization. Partly as a result,

81

the productivity decline during the 1969-1970 recession was more acute than during the recessionary periods of the late 1950s, despite the fact that these previous downturns were deeper. (See table 2.) The sharpest fall in productivity, however, took place during the recession of 1974-1975, when output per hour was depressed both by cyclical losses and by the energy shock. Econometric analysis of the world productivity slowdown at this time by Michael Bruno (1982) confirms that this phenomenon is explained largely by the combination of the energy shock and the contraction in output associated with the restrictive macroeconomic reaction.

To a substantial degree, the same process was repeated after the second OPEC shock in 1979-1980. This time, the world economy was moving less rapidly, while the feed-through of energy prices into domestic inflation rates was more gradual, producing a slower decline into recession. In part because of the slower pace of the contraction, labor markets adjusted more rapidly relative to the fall in demand, with the result that the recession brought smaller declines in productivity and greater increases in unemployment than in 1974-1975. By comparison, the speed of decline in the recession of the mid-1970s was so rapid that employment fell only with substantial lags causing a sharp initial decline in the output-labor ratio. The recession of 1980-1982 was considerably longer than that of 1974-1975, however; and

TABLE 2
Postwar Recessions

Cycle	Duration	Depth			
Peak to Trough	In Months	Decline in Real GNP	Decline in Industrial Production	Peak Jobless Rate	Trough Capacity Utilization
Nov. 1948–Oct. 49	11	−1.5%	− 9.4%	7.9%	71.7%
July 53–May 54	10	−3.2	−10.1	6.1	78.8
Aug. 57–Apr. 58	8	−3.3	−13.5	7.5	71.3
Apr. 60–Feb. 61	10	−1.2	− 8.6	7.1	73.5
Dec. 69–Nov. 70	11	−1.0	− 6.8	6.1	75.9
Nov. 73–Mar. 75	16	−4.6	−15.3	9.0	69.0
Jan. 80–July 80	6	−2.3	− 8.6	7.8	75.5
July 81–Nov. 82	16	−3.0	−12.3	10.8	68.8

Sources: National Bureau of Economic Research, Federal Reserve Board, Bureau of Labor Statistics, Commerce Department.

the cyclical decline in productivity at this time lasted for a period of roughly three years.

The contribution of cylical factors to the slowdown in productivity during the intervening recovery in 1975-1979 is less clear, but under-utilization of capacity appears to have played some role in other countries. The recovery of 1975-1979 was unusually slow in all of the industrial countries except the United States, where the looser stance of monetary policy enabled restoration of normal postwar growth rates in real GNP and a full recovery in capacity utilization. Nevertheless, while the U.S. economy had converged to full capacity by 1978, Canada, Japan, and Western Europe contined to experience substantial slack. The role of underutilization of capacity has been confirmed as an explanation for slower productivity growth in Canada and Western Europe (Helliwell, 1983; Lindbeck, 1983) but is largely irrelevant for the United States. Noncyclical factors therefore must account for some of the productivity decline.

The rise in oil costs is estimated to have accounted for as much as one-third of the cyclically-adjusted productivity slowdown in the United States since 1973. In addition to their direct impact on factor inputs of energy, the OPEC shocks had a secondary depressing effect on productivity through the capital-labor ratio and the output mix. The price increases raised the relative cost of capital inputs. At the same time, they encouraged shifts in the sectoral composition of output from energy-intensive manufacturing industries, which typically exhibit high productivity growth, to non-energy-intensive services where productivity growth rates tend to be slower.

Finally, several other factors explain the residual in the productivity decline. The demographic composition of the work force appears to have slowed productivity growth over the entire postwar period, although this factor was probably more important prior to the 1970s. Regulatory drag also has been an important factor, although estimates of the magnitude of regulations' effect have varied with the methodology used. The role of R&D in accounting for the productivity slowdown, on the other hand, is somewhat ambiguous, with the existing studies finding little demonstrable relationship.[3]

Research and Development

Trends in R&D spending reflect both cyclical movements in the economy and noncylical factors. Table 1 gives the annual rate of increase in outlays for R&D in constant dollars.

During the early 1960s, real R&D expenditures increased by 6.3 percent per year, a rapid rate of growth. Starting in the latter part of the decade, however, R&D spending slowed appreciably, to just over 2 percent per year in 1967-1968. This initial slowdown reflects in part slower growth and higher inflation. The Vietnam War and its diversion of military appropriations from R&D to purchase of equipment also played a part. The Vietnam War helps to explain the decline in R&D in 1969-1971, when growth rates were negative although the major cause appears to have been the recession of 1969-1970. Nevertheless, during the boom of 1971-1973, when much more rapid growth rates were achieved, R&D spending failed to improve as rapidly as during previous cyclical upswings in the economy. In 1973 at the peak of the boom, real R&D spending was still below its 1968 level. The partial recovery of R&D spending in 1972-1973 was especially weak in the private sector, apparently as a result of depressed profits. As documented in more detail below, during the recovery of the early 1970s, real after-tax profits failed to regain their peak levels of the mid-1960s, in part because of the effects of the 1971-1974 wage-price controls.

The recession of 1974-1975 led to another contraction in R&D spending. The recovery of 1976-1979 was associated with a major recovery in R&D expenditure but at roughly two points below the 6.3 percent annual rate experienced during the early 1960s. Although R&D grew more rapidly than overall economic activity during the early 1960s, it grew somewhat more slowly than real GNP in 1976-1979. On the other hand, R&D performance during the recessionary period 1980-1982 was by any standard unusually favorable, given the magnitude of the contraction in economic activity. This unusually strong growth may be related to provisions of the Economic Recovery Tax Act of 1981 aimed at enhancing research activity—a 25 percent tax credit for incremental R&D and a moratorium on Section 1.861-1.868 of the treasury regulations governing allocation of R&D expenses between the domestic branches of U.S. multinationals and their foreign subsidiaries.

Evidence, therefore, of both cyclical and secular behavior in R&D outlays exists. R&D allocations fluctuated in tandem with the business cycle, but the correlation here is somewhat weaker than for other economic indicators. Nevertheless, the prognosis reached in some studies that the United States has undergone a secular deterioration in R&D is not borne out.[4] A major component of the variation in R&D outlays reflects cyclical movements in profitability. The noncyclical factors are not altogether clear; but to the extent that they were related to one-time occurrences such as the Vietnam War and wage-price controls, the conclusion of a long-term decline is unjustified.

International Trade

A leading structuralist argument is that U.S. industry suffered a serious decline in international competitiveness in the 1970s. This argument rests on two major claims that the global market share of U.S. exports fell during the 1970s and that industrial country differentials in inflation and productivity growth placed the United States in an unfavorable relative cost position.

As has been pointed out on prior occasions, however, the allegation of loss in market share during the 1970s is factually incorrect. This claim was based primarily on the ratio of U.S. to world exports, measured in nominal dollar values, which underwent a cumulative decline of -8.7 percent between 1970 and 1980. Nevertheless, this decline reflects only the depreciation of the dollar that lowered the measured dollar value of exports at the same time as it raised the physical volume of exports. When world market shares are recalculated on the basis of the export volume rather than dollar export values, the U.S. share shows an increase rather than a decline during the decade. Moreover, when adjusted for differentials in the growth rates of the United States and other industrial countries, the U.S. world market share increased approximately 28 percent in the 1970s.[5]

The view that differentials in inflation and productivity caused a deterioration in competitiveness is also difficult to justify in view of the extremely unfavorable terms of trade that prevailed during the immediately preceding period of fixed exchange rates. Under the Bretton Woods regime, the dollar was seriously overvalued, and U.S. industry was fundamentally uncompetitive in world markets. Despite the fact that the United States had the highest absolute level of productivity at this time, the level of the dollar worked against any significant growth in exports and contributed to substantial import penetration. The result was that U.S. exports were limited for the most part to sectors in which the United States enjoyed an unequivocal comparative advantage, agriculture and high technology. The export-led business cycles characteristic of Western Europe and Japan in which dynamism was derived from durable manufactures facilitated by undervalued exchange rates were wholly absent in the United States. Instead, growth in the external sector during the Bretton Woods period was more typically based in the import multiplier.

By the same token, differentials in inflation and productivity growth are likely to affect relative cost positions only in a fixed exchange rate environment. The abandonment of the Bretton Woods system has made models of competitiveness based on changes in purchasing power parity largely obsolete. In a flexible exchange rate situation, factors such as relative price levels may have only a minimal impact on the determination of export performance because inflation and productivity differentials are likely to be offset by exchange rate variations. Further, recent economic theory on exchange rate determination has largely disconfirmed the older notion of purchasing power parity as a major cause of exchange rate movements. Instead, a series of factors—quantity theoretic relationships, portfolio balance mechanisms, etc., are likely to cause exchange rates to deviate substantially from their equilibrium (purchasing power parity) levels.[6] Real appreciation or real depreciation of exchange rates largely determines external competitiveness. Accordingly, U.S. competitiveness improved on average during the 1970s as a result of the dollar's depreciation. Table 3 gives the multilateral trade-weighted value of the dollar and the percent change in real exports, imports, and net exports for the period 1962 to 1983.

The behavior of international trade during the 1970s also reflects another major factor—differentials in aggregate demand. The role of differentials in demand in relative business cycles across national boundaries probably has not been accorded sufficient attention in the literature on international trade in view of its significance. During the Bretton Woods era, this factor tended to dominate the behavior of exports and imports. In the early stages of recoveries in the United States, exports tended to decline as production was redirected to meeting domestic demand, while increases in import penetration also were associated with higher domestic spending relative to aggregate demand overseas. After the initial recovery, higher growth in the United States normally accelerated the rate of expansion overseas and permitted faster export growth. From the Korean War up to the early 1970s, the United States went through this cycle approximately five times even though exports remained relatively sluggish because of the long-term overvaluation of the dollar.

During the Vietnam War escalation of the mid-1960s, differentials in demand between the United States and Western Europe led to substantial import penetration. The war escalation bid up demand for imports in the United States, while the prolonged recession in Germany lowered demand overseas and induced industrialists to shift toward export markets. Essentially the same process was repeated

TABLE 3

International Indicators

Year	Multilateral Trade-Weighted Value of the U.S. Dollar (March 1973 = 100)	Imports*	Exports*	Net Exports*
1962	N/A	11.00%	3.82%	−11.76%
1963	N/A	3.21	7.18	25.33
1964	N/A	5.37	12.28	36.17
1965	N/A	10.93	2.78	−21.09
1966	N/A	15.14	5.22	−35.64
1967	120.0	7.10	4.23	−16.92
1968	122.1	15.59	7.94	−64.81
1969	122.4	8.09	6.21	−52.63
1970	121.1	3.90	8.46	333.33
1971	117.8	4.05	0.71	−58.97
1972	109.1	10.68	9.15	−56.25
1973	99.1	6.65	25.55	2114.29
1974	101.4	−1.34	11.51	79.35
1975	98.5	−12.71	4.61	15.83
1976	105.6	18.63	6.38	−21.12
1977	103.3	7.32	2.54	−13.39
1978	92.4	12.98	12.22	9.09
1979	88.1	6.13	15.39	55.00
1980	87.4	−0.18	8.82	35.22
1981	102.9	7.26	0.38	−14.51
1982	116.6	1.46	−7.76	−32.79
1983	125.3	7.43	−5.70	−59.52

* Annual Percent Change

Source: Federal Reserve, Department of Commerce.

during the late 1970s. The import surge of 1976-1978 is accounted for primarily by the fact that the recovery in the United States was relatively strong while the recovery overseas was comparatively weak. Differentials in aggregate demand also partially explain the massive rise in import penetration in 1983-1984 when the U.S. economy exhibited unexpected strength while the other industrial countries experienced only sluggish growth.

With the transition to flexible exchange rates, the U.S. trade cycle became increasingly dependent on fluctuations in the dollar. The initial devaluation of the dollar in March 1973 was associated with a massive surge in export volume, which grew in real terms by over 25 percent; the speed of global economic expansion also contributed to the robustness of exports. Despite the fact that worldwide demand was growing more slowly during the late 1970s, the depreciation of the dollar in 1978-1980 produced a second major boom in exports, which grew by over 15 percent annually. The low level of the dollar in 1980 enabled exports to provide some relief from the recession that occurred that year. The appreciation of the dollar beginning in 1981, on the other hand, was substantially responsible for the loss in external competitiveness and contraction in exports during the early 1980s. Between its trough of 1980 and the second quarter of 1984, the dollar appreciated by over 50 percent on a multilateral trade-weighted basis.

The impact of exchange rate realignments on external competitiveness can be gauged through a comparison of unit labor costs across national boundaries. During the Bretton Woods period, the dollar's overvaluation caused unit costs in the United States to exceed those of the rest of the world. As a result of the dollar's depreciation during the 1970s, unit labor costs in the United States fell by 1979 to eighth place among the industrial countries, below those in the Scandinavian countries, Belgium, the Netherlands, Germany, and Switzerland. The appreciation of the dollar in 1981 restored U.S. unit labor costs to their historic position as the world's highest, according to Bureau of Labor Statistics estimates. Parenthetically, this exchange rate effect undercuts the view that productivity differentials in and of themselves significantly influenced competitiveness.

The international trade cycle has been slightly out of phase with the domestic business cycle to the extent that the major export surges generally have come at the end of periods of domestic expansion. In one critical respect, however, both the domestic business and international trade cycles have reflected the conduct of demand management policy. The import surges at the start of the business cycle resulted from shifts to reflation; the prolongation of the reflationary process led to depreciation in the exchange rate and export surges. In this sense, the behavior of international trade may be better explained as a function of business cycles and macroeconomic policy than of structural developments or secular changes in competitiveness.

Energy Shocks

Probably the most significant development affecting both the business cycle and the productive structure in the industrial countries since the mid-1970s has been the rise in energy costs caused by the OPEC oil price increases in 1973-1974 and 1979-1980. The OPEC shocks raised the price level directly because of the increases in input costs to production of energy-intensive goods. At the same time, they indirectly raised the underlying inflation rate, because they were followed by a general upward movement in wages aimed at maintaining real purchasing power. The adverse effects of the OPEC shocks on real output resulted from a transfer of purchasing power to the oil producing countries and a longer-term rise in the cost of inputs to production. Although a major result was a drop in inputs of energy, there were secondary effects on the output mix because of a shift in spending toward non-energy-intensive goods and services and on the capital stock because of the complementarity of energy and capital factor inputs.[7]

The implications of alternative monetary responses to the OPEC shocks have been critically analyzed in several theoretical studies.[8] Confronted with an increase in the relative cost of energy, policymakers face a choice between offsetting the shock through monetary restriction or attempting to maintain real output and employment through reflation. An accommodative response will yield higher output in the short run; but the underlying inflation rate will accelerate as wages rise and unit labor costs are marked up into prices. If the subsequent price increase also is accommodated and wages are effectively indexed, the inflation rate will accelerate to a continuously higher level. If the accommodative reaction takes place in a single country rather than the world economy at large, the trade deficit will increase with the differential in aggregate demand. If the currency is devalued, the increase in import prices will exacerbate inflationary pressures.

A restrictive response to the energy shock will cause a sharper contraction in output. Nevertheless, because of the resulting slack in labor markets, the rise in relative prices will not be fully transmitted to wages. The underlying rate of inflation will be therefore unchanged by the shock, and the increase in the short-term inflation rate will be transitory.

In short, the policy choice between offsetting or accommodating a supply shock is between a temporary loss in output with no long-term acceleration in inflation, on the one hand, and constant output gains with a higher underlying inflation rate on the other hand. U.S. monetary policy opted for the former, accounting for the greater depth of the recessionary periods from the mid-1970s onward.

There has been considerable debate as to the relative contributions of cyclical and structural factors to the rise in unemployment during the 1970s. The cyclical increases in unemployment attributable to downturns in the business cycle occurred at a time when expansion of the labor force was raising the underlying rate of unemployment.

The massive unemployment in 1980-1982 is generally acknowledged to be a cyclical phenomenon. At the trough of the 1981-1982 recession, slightly more than three-fifths of total measured unemployment consisted of job losses, with the remainder representing new entrants and reentrants to the labor force. Because the measured unemployment rate excluded discouraged workers, however, the official estimates may understate the cyclical component. Econometric tests also have indicated that the rise in unemployment resulted from deficient demand rather than labor force growth.[9]

Although the rise in unemployment in 1980-1982 was largely cyclical, its absolute level was extremely high, because the recessions came in the wake of massive increases in the labor force caused by the demographic boom that began at the end of World War II only tapered off in the early 1960s. (See table 4.) In large measure, the maturation of this generation accounted for the sharp increases in the labor force that followed in the decade 1969-1979. The labor force growth increased at twice the average of the previous decade, only partially as a result of changes in measurement techniques.

Perhaps a more important component of the labor force explosion of the 1970s was the increase in participation by women. Although the aggregate civilian labor force participation rate exhibits strong cyclical behavior, the male and female rates are strikingly different. The male participation rate has declined consistently since the early 1960s, with the exception of a two-year period in 1977-1978, largely as a consequence of the retirement of the earlier generation of male workers and the increased longevity of the retired age cohort. Conversely, the female participation rate increased consistently from the mid-1960s onward. Apart from a slowdown in 1970-1971, which seems to be a lagged result of the 1969-1970 recession, the rate of participation for women grew at an average rate of 1.7 percent per year.

The economy managed to absorb much of the influx of new workers. During the two major periods of economic expansion in the 1970s, increases in employment consistently surpassed their growth rate of the 1960s even though the unemployment rate remained at higher levels than in the 1960s. The extreme rapidity of the growth in employ-

TABLE 4

Demographic Indicators, 1962–1983 (Annual Percent Change)

| Year | Civilian Labor Force | Labor Force Participation Rate: | | | Civilian Employment |
		Total	Male	Female	
1962	0.21	−0.84	−1.09	−0.52	1.45
1963	1.73	−0.17	−0.73	1.06	1.59
1964	1.75	0.0	−0.49	1.04	2.28
1965	1.87	0.34	−0.37	1.55	2.57
1966	1.77	0.51	−0.37	2.54	2.54
1967	2.08	0.68	0.0	1.99	2.03
1968	1.80	0.0	−0.37	1.22	2.08
1969	2.54	0.84	−0.37	2.64	2.61
1970	2.52	0.50	−0.13	1.41	1.00
1971	1.95	−0.33	−0.75	0.23	0.88
1972	3.14	0.33	−0.25	1.15	3.51
1973	2.75	0.66	−0.13	1.82	3.54
1974	2.82	0.82	−0.13	2.24	2.03
1975	1.99	−0.16	−1.02	1.31	−1.09
1976	2.54	0.65	−0.51	2.16	3.39
1977	2.96	1.14	0.26	2.27	3.68
1978	3.27	1.44	0.26	1.24	4.38
1979	2.65	0.79	−0.13	1.80	2.89
1980	1.88	0.16	−0.51	1.81	0.48
1981	1.62	0.16	−0.52	1.71	1.10
1982	1.41	0.16	−0.52	0.96	−0.87
1983	1.19	0.16	−0.78	1.52	1.30

Source: Bureau of Labor Statistics.

ment helps account for two widely noted adverse trends, the acceleration in the underlying inflation rate and the decline in cyclically adjusted productivity growth. On two occasions, in 1972-1973 and 1978-1979, the stimulative posture of demand management policy caused the unemployment rate to fall below its equilibrium level, triggering an acceleration in wages. At the same time, the rapid employment gains caused stagnation or decline in the capital-labor ratio, notwithstanding rapid growth in business fixed investment in the recovery periods.

Conclusions

This brief review of structural versus cyclical arguments is not definitive, but it does underscore the need to examine the business cycle and its determinants to understand the trends in industrial performance. Much of the structural adjustment literature has failed to distinguish secular from cyclical phenomena and has confused structural changes with exacerbated cyclical fluctuations. Even a cursory review of the data reveals that cyclical interpretations possess considerable power in explaining major economic developments during the 1970s. A more systematic analysis of cyclical patterns and their determinants—that is, the conduct of demand management policy—is therefore in order.

Macroeconomic Policy and the Business Cycle

The Business Cycle in Retrospect

The period from the early 1970s onward is marked by the increasing magnitude of business cycle fluctuations. Following a prolonged growth phase during the 1960s, the economy had two major booms, in 1971-1973 and 1975-1979, both of which registered growth rates comparable to or higher than those of previous postwar expansions. Like the Vietnam War boom of the late 1960s, the two growth spurts of the 1970s were accompanied by highly reflationary macroeconomic policies. As a result, they were characterized by substantial acceleration in inflation and the emergence of considerable financial instability toward the end of the business cycle. Moreover, the booms were interrupted by major recessions in 1974-1975 and 1980-1982, which in both depth and duration were the most acute of the postwar era. (See table 4.)

By almost every benchmark, the recessions were unusually severe. The recession of 1974-1975 witnessed the sharpest peak to trough declines in GNP and industrial production of the postwar period and represented the longest (16 months) cyclical contraction recorded up to this time. In terms of output losses, the recessions of 1980 and 1981-1982 were somewhat shallower, although the cumulative increases in unemployment and declines in capacity utilization represented postwar records. What is distinctive about the 1980-1982 period is the extraordinary duration of the cyclical decline. Because the two recessions were separated only by an abortive 12-month recovery, the overall recessionary period lasted roughly three years. Moreover, the 1980 recession was preceded by a pronounced growth slowdown in 1979 in the wake of the second OPEC shock; the recovery in 1983 did not begin until the spring quarter. Compared with after postwar downturns, the extended recession is so atypical that some writers have characterized it as a minor depression.

The 1974-1975 and 1980-1982 recessions also are distinguished by the degree to which they were worldwide. Earlier postwar slowdowns were not by and large global in scale. The recessions of the 1950s were considerably milder overseas than in the United States. The major Western European recession of the mid-1960s was missed completely in North America, while the global slowdown in 1969-1971 emerged at different times across national boundaries.

The origins of these massive cyclical swings in the U.S. and global economies are related to corresponding shifts in macroeconomic policy. The first expansion-contraction cycle lasting from 1971 to 1975 was accompanied initially by simultaneous reflation throughout the industrial countries, which led to a global boom and a rapid acceleration in the world inflation rate, exacerbated by the rise in OPEC oil prices. The simultaneous shift to restraint in 1974 caused the recession to become worldwide. The longer cycle lasting from 1975 to 1982 was less reflationary worldwide, although monetary policies were exceedingly stimulative in the United States. As in 1974, the shift to restraint was triggered by the second OPEC shock in 1979-1980. The ensuing restrictive nature of monetary policy in the United States prolonged the recession. This led to a major exchange rate realignment that acted as a constraint on the ability of the other industrial countries to pursue countercyclical policies.

The 1971-1975 Cycle

The Vietnam War escalation during the late 1960s produced both the longest single period of sustained expansion in the U.S. economy and the first major acceleration in inflation since the Korean War. Although inflation remained stable at an underlying rate in the 1 percent range during the first half of the decade, by 1966, as the economy reached full capacity and labor markets exhibited increasing tightness, a two-point increase was recorded. The emergence of greater inflationary pressure in the latter part of the decade resulted from the Johnson administration's decision to finance the war through larger deficits rather than through a tax increase. Although the Federal Reserve initially responded with restraint in 1966, in 1967-1968 the thrust of both fiscal and monetary policy became expansionist, with the federal deficit peaking at 3 percent of GNP. By 1968 the inflation rate had accelerated into the 5 percent range.[10]

Starting in the final months of the year and continuing for the first two years of the Nixon administration, fiscal and monetary policy reverted to a disinflationary posture. The results were equivocal, however; the recession of 1969-1970 achieved no immediate deceleration in inflation, which stabilized at 5 percent annually. The rise in unemployment and the seeming imperviousness of inflation to the restrictive policies, combined with the initial weakness of the recovery in 1971, caused the Nixon administration to completely reevaluate its economic strategy that year. The New Economic Program (NEP) launched in August imposed wage-price controls to reduce inflation. Simultaneously, both monetary and fiscal policy went over to sustained expansion.

Diverse political motives have been imputed to the NEP, a remarkably Keynesian economic program for an ostensibly conservative administration. The "election year cycle" frequently has been cited as a motive.[11] The Nixon administration confronted a difficult political situation in 1971, raising the incentives to augment its chances of reelection by suppressing inflation through controls while restoring high employment by raising demand. The Republicans, with minorities in both Houses of Congress, had lost nine House seats in the 1970 off-year election. In addition to economic management, the administration was widely perceived to be vulnerable over the Vietnam War issue. The economic issue was compounded by the exceptionally favorable economic performance recorded during the 1960s, when expansion had been sustained for eight years. As a result of this experience, economists had overestimated the ability of activist demand management policies to provide sustained growth and full employment without price instability. Judged by the criteria of the performance of the 1960s and the prevailing beliefs about slope of the short-run Phillips curve, the failure of the gradualist disinflationary program of 1969-1970 created powerful incentives for a change of course to one that would supress inflation through controls while restoring high employment by raising demand. The fact that the international situation in 1971 argued for a continuation of the restrictive policies reinforces the political interpretation of the NEP. Since the late 1960s when the rise in imports engendered by the Vietnam War had led to sizable reserve outflows through the current account, the dollar had been seriously overvalued and by 1971 had come under considerable speculative pressure.

94

Nevertheless less self-interested considerations may also have been at work. Although the rise in unemployment in 1969-1970 was due in part to structural factors, this was not widely recognized at the time. The view that the rise in unemployment was largely cyclical evidently led policymakers to overestimate the degree of slack in the economy and underestimate the inflationary implications of the NEP. At the same time, the failure of inflation to decelerate in the face of tighter fiscal and monetary policies was attributed to union militancy, suggesting the need for wage restraints. The perception that demand was inadequate while inflation was dominated by structual inertia in wage settlements provided a convincing rationale to achieve a more favorable inflation-unemployment trade-off through controls. The NEP may therefore have been impelled in part by Phillips curve considerations rather than solely through narrow reelection motives.

The effect of the NEP was to throw the economy into a major reflationary boom. From the last quarter of 1971 through the end of the first quarter of 1973, industrial production, manufacturing output, and capital investment accelerated at close to their peak rates of the postwar era. The surge in growth was fueled primarily by consumer spending, concentrated in housing and durables. The surge in aggregate demand, propelled by the expansionary thrust of monetary policy, also led to a major accumulation in inventories. The boom also engendered a sharp rise in inflation. Initially, the controls were effective against both wages and prices; deflecting the price level downward by an estimated -1.4 to -1.6 percentage points.[12] By mid-1972, however, successful legal challenges to the wage standards by major unions had restored wages to levels they would have reached in the absence of controls. Thereafter, the controls worked to compress profit margins.[13] Despite the fact that the controls continued to depress the price level until late 1973, the inflation rate accelerated continuously from mid-1972 onward. Inflation was accentuated not only by the strength of demand but also by the abandonment of fixed exchange rates in March 1973. The devaluation of the dollar at this time raised import prices and exports. The latter aggravated domestic price pressures associated with agricultural and raw material shortages.

The U.S. reflation of the early 1970s, on the heels of the Vietnam War escalation, is generally credited with the breakdown of the Bretton Woods fixed exchange rate system. Substantial downward pressure on the dollar had emerged during the late 1960s when the Vietnam War trade deficits produced substantial reserve outflows. After repeated unsuccessful attempts to defend the dollar, the Nixon administration in August 1971 suspended gold convertibility and allowed a minimal devaluation. The basic elements of the Bretton Woods system were temporarily preserved by the Smithsonian Agreements of December 1971. Nevertheless, as major currencies were revalued to correct the misalignments that had developed under Bretton Woods, substantial variation in exchange rates took place the following year. With the devaluation of the dollar in March 1973, the fixed exchange rate system collapsed entirely.

Another distinctive feature of the 1971-1973 boom was its world-wide character. Almost all of the industrial countries pursued reflationary policies simultaneously and caused the expansionary cycle to extend across national boundaries. Expansionist monetary policy worldwide was partially the result of developments in the United States. As a consequence of the trade deficits engendered by the Vietnam War and reserve outflows through the current account, world liquidity exploded during the early 1970s. Total global liquidity, overwhelmingly consisting of dollar reserves, increased by over 20 percent in 1970, 1972, and 1973, and by close to 40 percent in 1971. This massive increase in reserves contributed to the reflationary stance of macroeconomic policy overseas, albeit through a somewhat indirect mechanism. The proximate effect of the growth in dollar liquidity was that by 1971 most of the other industrial countries were experiencing large balance of payments surpluses and reserve inflows. Under the circumstances, attempts to control the rise in liquidity through restrictive domestic monetary policies would have been at least partially offset by countervailing reserve movements.[14] With sterilization of the reserve flows therefore effectively precluded as a policy option, countries typically tried to restore balance of payments equilibrium through reflation. In short, other industrial countries allowed their domestic monetary policies to become expansionist in order to mitigate reserve movements that were not amenable to control through domestic restriction.[15]

Reflationary policies accelerated not only worldwide economic expansion but also the global inflation rate. Unlike the inflation rise of the late 1960s, a function primarily of wage increases in tight labor markets, the price volatility of the early 1970s was more a function of demand pressures in global markets exacerbated by shortages of key raw materials and commodities. By 1973 it had become apparent that the world economy was overheating, and demand management policies began shifting away from stimulus in a belated effort to cool off the boom. At this juncture, however, the 400 percent increase in world oil prices boosted the short-term inflation rate as did the wage-price rebound following removal of controls in the United States and the

United Kingdom.[16] By 1974, the inflation rate for the industrial countries averaged over 13 percent; in some countries the rate was upwards of 25 percent.

Macroeconomic policies shifted sharply to restraint to control the burst of inflation. In the United States and elsewhere both monetary and fiscal policy became restrictive, with monetary policy bearing the main burden. The resulting decline in demand took place at a time when inventories were pervasively overbuilt, with the result that the industrial economies simultaneously slipped into recession led by inventory reduction. Two other factors contributed to the extreme depth of the 1974-1975 downturn. The first OPEC shock forced a sharp fall in domestic spending because of the transfer of purchasing power to the oil-producing countries; at the same time, the rise in oil prices accentuated the decline in output, particularly in energy-intensive manufacturing industries, by causing a reduction in factor inputs of energy. Secondly, the simultaneous shift to restraint in the industrial countries meant that the decline in demand was transmitted across national boundaries through the channel of trade flows. The contraction in demand for exports worked against a major countercyclical role for international trade.

Despite the severity of the downturn, governments by and large did not undertake any countercyclical stimulus until the later stages of the recession. In the United States, the stubbornness of the inflation rate caused the restrictive monetary stance to be maintained until the first quarter of 1975. Only as the inflation rate decelerated did the Federal Reserve revert to expansion and Congress enacted a series of tax cuts and other expansionary fiscal measures.[17] Most of the other industrial countries adopted countercyclical measures somewhat earlier, although there, too, high inflation prevented demand management from becoming systematically reflationary. By the second quarter of 1975, nevertheless, the recession had passed its trough and the world economy was moving into recovery.

The 1975-1982 Cycle

The initial recovery, commencing in the United States in the spring of 1975, was led by a reversal of the inventory cycle following the loosening of fiscal and monetary policy. Despite the depth of the downturn, the recovery was exceedingly rapid; consumer spending and inventory accumulation raised real output at rates well within the norm for postwar expansions. Meanwhile, as the effects of the OPEC

price rise were exhausted, inflation slowed by one-half to an underlying rate of slightly over 5 percent.

To a considerable degree, restrictive monetary policy in 1974 had
limited the effect of the energy shock to a one-time increase in the
price level and prevented it from translating into a rise in the underlying inflation rate. In the other industrial countries also, the rate of
inflation during the recovery of the late 1970s depended in large
measure on the reaction of monetary policy to the OPEC shock. In
the countries that had adopted restrictive strategies, the inflation rate
in 1976 was generally no higher than and frequently lower than prior
to the OPEC crisis. Conversely, in countries that attempted reflationary
solutions to the oil crisis in order to maintain full employment or
resorted to countercyclical stimulus of monetary policy, the reverse
occurred. Canada, France, Italy and the United Kingdom emerged
from the recession with average inflation rates higher than those prevailing before the shock. The United States, Japan, and West Germany, on the other hand, had reduced their inflation rates and were
in a better position to achieve sustainable recoveries without renewed
price volatility.[18]

Even in the countries where inflation rates had declined, however,
the policymakers faced the problem of avoiding a recurrence of the
overheating that had characterized the previous recovery. To this end,
the use of quantitative targets for monetary aggregates represented
an important innovation in demand management. To some extent,
the speed of monetary expansion in 1971-1973 was due to central
bank targeting of nominal interest rates in an inflationary environment; holding rates to historic norms had required greater reflation
than anticipated. Under the new approach, central banks did not
abandon pegging interest rates in the short term but placed greater
emphasis on annual money supply targets.

Although the Federal Reserve adopted formal quantitative targets
beginning in 1976, monetary policy in the United States remained
almost continuously expansionary until the end of 1979. M1 (the
money supply: money in circulation and current accounts at banks)
was held within its target range of 4.5 percent to 7.5 percent in 1976;
but the accession of the Carter administration led to a shift toward
more systematic reflation. The Carter administration inherited a massive increase in unemployment as a result of the 1974-1975 recession
and demographic increases in the labor force. Raising employment
required a more expansionist course for demand management that in
turn implied deviation from the Federal Reserve's monetary targets.
The Carter administration evidently assumed that inflation would

remain stable in the 5 percent to 6 percent range, while monetary expansion at stable velocity would produce a normal GNP growth rate of 11 percent and real growth of 5 percent per year. M1 accelerated to over 8 percent annually in 1977-1978, well above the Federal Reserve's target of 4.5 percent to 6.5 percent. Not until late 1979 was the average rate of money growth brought within the upper limit of the target range.[19] The increases in nominal GNP also were higher than anticipated.

Under the reflationary strategy the United States achieved higher growth, relative to trend, than the other industrial countries in the late 1970s. The GNP and industrial production rose as rapidly in 1975-1979 as in previous recoveries. In other industrial countries real growth rates were considerably lower than historical norms, but in the United States the rebound produced the largest increases in industrial and manufacturing output since the recovery of 1959 and the highest real increases in investment since the Korean War. Industrial output growth was slightly higher on average (6.69 percent per year) than during the 1971-1973 boom (6.44 percent) and the expansion of 1961-1969 (6.60 percent). U.S. heavy industry performance was far superior to that of the other advanced economies. In Western Europe, the recovery of 1975-1979 was atypically weak with growth rates below their postwar trends. In Japan, the rate of real GNP growth was only half that of the 1960s. By 1978, capacity utilization had fully recovered in the United States; elsewhere, there was still evidence of pervasive slack.[20]

Reflation in the United States also entailed a substantial depreciation in the exchange rate, a function again primarily of monetary policy. As a result of a faster rate of money creation in the United States and reserve outflows through the current account, dollar liquidity in world markets grew rapidly while demand for dollars increased more gradually. Surplus dollar liquidity was largely responsible for causing the exchange rate to undershoot purchasing power parity. The dollar's decline was probably reinforced by expectations abroad. Reflationary monetary policy coupled with the expansionary fiscal posture in 1978 undermined investor confidence and led a shift of assets into stronger currencies such as the German mark and Swiss franc. The following year loss of confidence was compounded by the second rise in oil prices, the Iran hostage crisis, and the apparent political weakness of the Carter administration. In large measure, this explains why the exchange rate remained low in 1980, notwithstanding the sharp deceleration in the money supply and the rise in interest rates. By comparison, the acceleration in U.S. inflation, producing a major inflation differential with Japan and West Germany (although not Western Europe as a whole), is not a fully convincing explanation of the dollar's decline. Causality tests indicate that causation runs almost exclusively from the exchange rate to inflation and that the prices of movements exert only a minimal impact on exchange rates.[20]

The expansionary stance of macroeconomic policy during the 1970s was nevertheless associated with a substantial buildup in the inflation rate. Several factors were responsible for the increase in inflation. The exchange rate depreciation itself accounts for a significant component, not only because of the direct rise in import costs but more importantly because of the influence of international prices on domestic wage-price cycles.[21] The high growth rate of the economy was associated with a substantial tightening of labor markets and the emergence of widespread capacity constraints. By the latter part of 1978, the unemployment rate had declined to the 6 percent range. Given the demographic growth of the labor force during the 1970s, this was roughly equal to its natural rate.[22] The following year the unemployment rate fell below its natural rate, implying a substantial increase in wage pressures. Similarly, by 1979 the capacity utilization rate in manufacturing surpassed 87 percent, comparable to the levels experienced during the prior acceleration in inflation in 1973 and at the height of the Vietnam War. By the more technical measure of output ratio (the ratio of actual to potential GNP), the U.S. economy was operating at full capacity during the late 1970s, while real growth rates were substantially above rates consistent with price stability.[23] In essence, the economy moved to the upper end of its short-run Phillips curve in the late 1970s. The inflation rate had undergone a major acceleration even before the second OPEC shock. Although the dramatic rise in consumer prices in 1979-80 reflected in part the increasing relative energy costs, the underlying rate of inflation as measured by the average growth rate of unit labor costs also rose substantially.

In the face of increasing inflationary pressure and financial instability the Carter administration in October 1979 finally abandoned its commitment to full employment and shifted to a disinflationary strategy. As in 1973, the shift to restriction was worldwide; in response to the second increase in oil prices, the industrial countries simultaneously adopted restrictive measures to offset the rise in inflation and mitigate pressure on the balance of payments.

The recession that emerged in the first half of 1980 in the United States is distinguished not only by its unusual brevity but also by the fact that it was led by a decline in retail sales rather than by inventory reduction. A major liquidation in stocks took place in 1979, in anticipation of an earlier recession, so that the inventory-sales ratio was relatively low in 1980. Inventories moved countercyclically during the recession and partially mitigated the output losses.[24] More important, the course of the economy in 1980 reflected continued changes in macroeconomic policy—the imposition of credit controls in March and their termination along with a short-lived shift to reflation during the second half. Output losses were concentrated in the second quarter; the economy moved into a brief recovery under the impact of greater monetary stimulus in the second half.

Unlike the 1980 recession, which was widely anticipated, the second recession starting in mid-1981 was unexpected, and its extreme duration and depth were underestimated. The pattern of decline, led by inventory reduction, was more conventional, although the appreciation of the dollar produced more severe output losses in external trade. Probably the most distinctive feature of the 1981-1982 recession, however, was the mix of demand management. Monetary policy in 1981 was exceedingly restrictive, with the major aggregates actually undershooting their target ranges; and the restrictive stance was maintained throughout the first half of 1982.[25] Not until the second half of the year did the Federal Reserve move aggressively to lower interest rates and allow the monetary aggregates to overshoot their targets. To some degree, the shift was forced on the central bank by the emergence of the Third World debt crisis.[26] Nevertheless, unlike the restrictive fiscal actions taken in previous recessions, fiscal policy became increasingly expansionist from 1981 onward. The full employment budget began showing unprecedented deficits.

This asymmetric mix of macroeconomic policy was less the result of clearly defined stabilization goals than a function of ideological commitments by the Reagan administration, which putatively rejected short-run demand management as a policy objective. The effects of monetary restriction and fiscal expansion have been the subject of considerable debate. On the one hand, the tax reductions appear to have exerted some countercyclical influence through income-expenditure flows. Econometric simulations by Allen Sinai (1983) suggest that in the absence of the ERTA-TEFRA tax changes the 1981-1982 output losses during the 1981-1982 recession would have been greater by roughly one percentage point of GNP.[27] Furthermore, the fiscal stimulus implied by full employment deficits exceeding 3 percent of GNP contributed to the speed of economic expansion during the 1983-1984 recovery. Nevertheless, the expansionist fiscal posture also contributed to the increase in the average level of real interest rates and the appreciation of the dollar.

101

The output losses during the 1981-1982 recession were made significantly worse by the appreciation of the dollar starting in the second quarter of 1981.

The realignment in exchange rates resulted primarily from portfolio balance mechanisms. Because of the rise in real interest rates in the United States, the inflation-adjusted rate of return on dollar-denominated financial assets exceeded rates of return overseas. The resulting shift of asset portfolios overseas into dollars and the inflows of international reserves caused the exchange rate's appreciation. Independently of its effect on the real interest rate, expansionary fiscal policy accentuated the realignment through the increased volume of Treasury securities issued on international markets and the increased share of the deficit financed through reserve inflows. The fact that the stock market boom of 1982-1983 preceded the worldwide recovery also raised the rate of return on U.S. corporate equity in the United States relative to rates of return on equity overseas. Apparent political stability and conservatism in the United States help restore confidence in the dollar as a "safe haven."

In addition to their domestic economic consequences, the Reagan administration's macroeconomic policies aggravated and prolonged the worldwide recession of 1980-1982. Restrictive monetary reaction to the OPEC crisis led the world economy into recession in 1980. By 1981 the rise in energy costs was largely exhausted, but the dollar's appreciation dealt a second blow to the global economy. The rise in the dollar exchange rate caused further increases in import costs in the other industrial countries, particularly in dollar-denominated oil prices. Simultaneously, the real interest rate differential between the United States and the other industrial countries generated reserve flows into dollar-denominated assets and undercut the external balance in Western Europe and Japan. Most countries felt compelled to apply restrictive policies to mitigate the interest rate differential, support the balance of payments, and prevent further depreciation of their exchange rates. Countries that attempted countercyclical stimulus experienced reserve losses followed by depreciation crises and increases in their inflation rates; they were obliged to abandon reflation and revert to restrictive measures. Overall, the level of U.S. interest rates and the dollar exchange rate caused a global shift to deflation, contributing to output losses and increases in unemployment unprecedented for the postwar era.

The 1983-1984 Recovery

In the wake of the 1981-1982 recession, initial projections were for only a weak recovery in 1983. Beginning in the second quarter, however, the economy rebounded sharply and continued to expand for the next 12 months. Demand and industrial output increased at rates well within the postwar average; employment gains actually exceeded the norm. The recovery's speed was a product of aggressively expansionary fiscal policy coupled with the more stimulative monetary posture taken in the second half of 1982. During the last two quarters of that year, interest rates dropped approximately 600 basis points, while the monetary aggregates consistently surpassed the upper limit of their target ranges.[28]

The recovery was led in its initial stages by resurgent consumer spending and renewed inventory investment. Although in real terms consumer spending fell somewhat short of its growth rates during the recoveries of the 1970s, its robustness in 1983 was remarkable in view of the high level of real interest rates. Several factors temporarily outweighed the effect of interest rates. Greater consumer liquidity was a major contributor. After drawing down their financial assets to acquire durable goods during the reflationary environment of the late 1970s, consumers managed to reliquify in the subsequent recessionary period. Thus, in 1983 they were able to spend heavily without risking excessive leveraging. Pent-up demand also played a role. In the 1980 and 1981-1982 recessions, consumers deferred purchases of durables until expectations adjusted to the reality of a falling unemployment rate in early 1983. At that point, the rise in spending was concentrated in the durable goods industries that had experienced the sharpest declines in output. The strength of longer run demographic factors, especially the increases in the population aged 25 to 35 that tends to dissave to acquire housing and durables, further strengthened demand. Finally, the more reflationary monetary stance meant that increased availability of credit partially offset the high cost of borrowing.

Inventory behavior has been less typical. Although the shift from decumulation to rebuilding contributed to the recovery, inventories were held unusually low relative to demand. The inventory-sales ratio fell almost continuously until early 1984. Not only did high interest rates raise the real cost of carrying inventory, but severe corporate illiquidity also induced business to protect its cash flow by liquidating surplus stocks. A second factor has to do with diminished inflationary expectations. The massive inventory buildups of 1973, 1977-1978 and, to a lesser extent, 1981 were predicated on the expectation of continuous increases in demand and increases in the real rate of return on inventories associated with rising retail prices. Once expectations adjusted to greater price stability, they no longer worked in favor of inventory accumulation. Uncertainty about the duration of economic expansion reinforced the more cautious stockbuilding strategy.[29] The inventory situation also reflected the impact of volatility in demand over the previous few years. The massive demand fluctuations in 1980-1983 made it increasingly difficult for business to gauge the correct level of stocks relative to sales, and losses in profitability caused by overbuilding made it necessary to hold inventories low to minimize the risk of unanticipated surpluses.

The recovery also was marked by the continued appreciation of the dollar, a reversal of the cyclical pattern of the 1970s when recoveries were associated with devaluations. The transition to a more stimulative monetary policy and the reduction in interest rates in late 1982 were widely expected to lower the exchange rate but for a variety of reasons failed to do so. As other industrial countries responded to the decline in U.S. interest rates with countercyclical loosening moves, the real interest rate differential remained fairly constant. At the same time, in the wake of the second rise in OPEC oil prices and the increases in dollar-denominated import costs associated with exchange rate realignment, world demand for dollar reserves grew more rapidly than expected. The emergence of the debt crisis and the LDCs' need for additional reserve inflows further raised the demand for dollar liquidity. As a result, the dollar continued to rise until early 1984.

By the second half of 1984 there were indications of slowdown in economic activity. The possibility of an early recession in 1985 appears remote; both the stance of fiscal policy and the absence of inflationary pressures for monetary restraint militate against a serious downturn. The inflation rate will remain moderate because of continued slack in labor markets and the continued strength of the dollar, keeping import costs low and maintaining slack in export industries that have lost competitiveness. The growth rate is likely to be subnormal in 1985, but a return to the price instability that accompanied the recoveries of the 1970s will be avoided. In the external sector, the major risk is less one of sharp dollar depreciation than of long-term overvaluation. With the current mix of demand management policies, interest rate differentials may continue to offset the widening deficit in the trade accounts. The net result would be a long-term loss in competitiveness and a corresponding rise in import penetration.

Macroeconomic Policy in Retrospect

In retrospect, macroeconomic policy has tended on average to be destabilizing since the late 1960s. In particular, demand management has exhibited a procyclical bias. Stimulus sustained until fairly late in the business cycle prolonged expansion but also caused the economy to overheat and led to an acceleration in inflation. Greater price volatility in turn compelled macroeconomic policy to shift to restraint until a sufficient deceleration in inflation had been achieved but at the cost of exacerbating the resulting recessions.

This procyclical bias has characterized both fiscal and monetary policy. The full employment budget initially went into disequilibrium in the late 1960s, despite the fact that a more restrictive fiscal posture would have been appropriate to the Keynesian demand management strategy ostensibly followed by the Johnson administration. Similarly, a countercyclical fiscal strategy would have required a more restrictive posture during the successive booms of the 1970s. Nevertheless, the full employment deficit surpassed 2 percent of the GNP in 1972 and 1977-1978, with the result that stimulus contributed to the overheating of the economy on both occasions. Fiscal policy only reverted to restraint at the end of the business cycle, according to the low full employment deficits recorded in 1974 and 1979-1980. The delay in the transition to fiscal restraint until the economy was already poised on the verge of a slowdown merely served to exacerbate the ensuing recession.

The same procyclical fiscal expansion characteristic of the booms of the late 1960s and 1970s has been practiced in more extreme form since 1981. The Reagan administration's budget deficits are fundamentally noncyclical in origin. Even if the economy reaches full employment by the end of the decade, the deficit will be reduced only a little. Instead, the increasing structural component of the deficit will progressively offset the cyclical component; and by the end of the 1980s, the full employment deficit will reach 4 percent of the GNP.[30] In the long run, the major effect of the Reagan administration's budgetary program will be marked fiscal disequilibrium.

Monetary policy has exhibited an even more pronounced procyclical bias. The massive monetary expansion of 1972-1973 far exceeded the requirements of recovery from the 1969-1970 recession. The short-term growth rate reached levels that could not be sustained. In 1974-1975, monetary policy erred in the opposite direction; it aggravated the cyclical contraction without slowing the jump in inflation largely induced by the oil shock. The country avoided an even deeper recession in part because increases in monetary velocity mitigated the Federal Reserve's restrictive posture. The reflationary policies of the late 1970s were sustained beyond the normal length of postwar business cycles notwithstanding the slide in the dollar and the acceleration in inflation in 1978. The disinflationary policies of 1981-1982 were also more restrictive than needed to meet the original monetary targets, and thus in time were accompanied by declining velocity.

The change in course since mid-1982 has been the object of considerable controversy, prompting fears in some circles of renewed inflation. By and large, the Federal Reserve largely has adhered to its target ranges and has adopted countercyclical measures aimed at slowing the pace of expansion. Far from engaging in systematic reflation, the Federal Reserve appears to have worked out a more effective countercyclical policy.

If monetary policy has in fact become more stabilizing since 1982, the cyclical volatility associated with the reflation-disinflation cycles of the 1970s may be avoided in the 1980s. This does not mean that the United States has resolved the problems inherent in an asymmetric mix of demand management policies. The central problem for policymakers in the 1980s may not be cyclical volatility as much as chronic fiscal imbalance, a quasi-permanent loss in competitiveness and below average long-term growth stemming from chronically high real interest rates and a corresponding misalignment in exchange rates.

Policy Implications

Why Macroeconomic Policies Were Destabilizing

The procyclical bias in macroeconomic policy since the late 1960s is attributable to a combination of factors. External shocks and domestic structural changes have played a role; political influences also have been important. Political analyses of demand management, however, are divided between interpretations that have emphasized secular forces such as institutional pressures on fiscal outlays and discretionary policy changes reflecting the priorities of successive administrations.

In the fiscal area, there may be some role for structural pressures. Discretionary policies such as the Vietnam War escalation and the Great Society programs led to the initial fiscal disequilibrium; but during the next decade the expansionary stance of fiscal policy owed more to the growth of transfer payments and income security programs. On this basis, some writers have identified an institutional bias toward higher spending. Empirical studies have found little evidence in favor of such exclusively institutional interpretations, however.[31] Nevertheless the "spending bias" hypothesis has found little support in empirical studies and does not explain the restrictive turns in fiscal policy in 1969-1970, 1974, and 1979-1980. Fiscal policy up to the 1970s also must be understood as a function of stabilization goals. Excessive stimulus during recoveries represented an effort to raise employment, while the periodic shifts to restriction resulted from an effort to attack inflation.

The growth of the structural deficit under the Reagan administration owes more to political priorities, the ERTA tax cuts and the military buildup, than to institutional constraints. The increased debt service costs associated with high interest rates were largely unanticipated. The administration apparently had excessive confidence in the ability of the alleged effects of marginal tax rates on the structure of incentives to offset the effects of monetary disinflation. As a result, the economic forecasts on which the administration's fiscal policies were based turned out to be badly off-target.[32] The overly stimulative fiscal stance stemmed in part from a failure to gauge the macroeconomic implications of simultaneous fiscal stimulus and monetary restraint.

The procyclical bias in monetary policy had less to do with ideological factors than with stabilization goals. Nor was it primarily a result of fiscal deficits. Although some studies have argued that monetary policy tended to accommodate fiscal impulses, this does not fully account for the behavior of monetary aggregates.[33] The initial rise in inflation after 1966 can be traced to monetary ratification of the Vietnam War deficits. During the 1970s and early 1980s, however, the fiscal-monetary relationship became progressively asymmetric.[34] Far from merely reacting to fiscal pressures, monetary policy appears to be driven by autonomous stabilization goals.

There is abundant evidence that the OPEC shocks induced a significant offsetting monetary reaction. Prolonged monetary restriction during the recessionary periods is also explained in part by the effects of the OPEC crises on the inflation rate. A second structural factor that worked in the opposite direction was the demographic explosion of the labor force. As the labor force expanded, monetary policy repeatedly went over to stimulus to raise employment. The operating procedures of the Federal Reserve also have been faulted in allowing excessive monetary volatility over the cycle. The monetarist critique that the traditional procedure of pegging interest rates would be likely to work against effective control over monetary aggregates in an inflationary environment, appears to have some validity for the two reflationary periods of the 1970s. Keynesians have criticized the Federal Reserve for unnecessarily prolonging the 1982 recession by overstaying its adherence to monetary targets in the face of declining velocity. Operating procedures may account for some of the major developments in the monetary sector, but a more significant question is how political factors account for the choice of stabilization targets and, indirectly, the choice of operating procedures. To a large extent, the Federal Reserve's selection of stabilization targets reflects the orientation of the administration in power. Under Democratic administrations, macroeconomic policy primarily was oriented toward reducing unemployment; under Republican administrations, greater priority was attached to control of inflation.[35] Although monetary policy under the Johnson administration was linked inextricably to the Vietnam War, higher unemployment was not accepted as a necessary cost of reducing inflation in 1967-1968. During the Carter administration, policies were consistently reflationary until the second OPEC shock. Under Nixon in 1969-1970, Nixon and Ford in 1974-1975, and Reagan in 1981-1982, monetary policy was aimed primarily at controlling inflation, notwithstanding its substantial output and unemployment costs. The Nixon administration's NEP represents the sole major exception to this pattern.

In sum, no single factor accounts for the procyclical orientation of U.S. macroeconomic policy and the resulting destabilization of the business cycle. Instead, these were the product of several unrelated factors: the timing of changes in administrations, the Vietnam War, the expansion of the labor force, and the successive OPEC crises. To the degree that diverse one-time events shaped the conduct of stabilization policy, there is nothing inevitable about the procyclicalism that has characterized the last two decades. In a more favorable global economic environment, in which energy prices remain stable and labor force growth slows down as projected, monetary policy may well prove less destabilizing. On the other hand, to the extent that structural fiscal deficit remains large, fiscal policy will continue to work against business cycle stability during the 1980s.

Policy Alternatives

The experiments in monetary and fiscal policy over the last five years have sharpened the debate among competing macroeconomic schools and undermined the consensus that existed before the policy changes were undertaken. The controversies, especially over the control of monetary aggregates and changes in tax rates, are too extensive to be resolved here.[36] Instead, this conclusion is confined to a number of observations on the alternatives now under consideration for future policy actions.

In the monetary area, critics of the New Federal Reserve Policy have argued that changes in definition and unstable velocity make monetary aggregates poor indicators of real economic activity. Despite the well-publicized distortions in monetary measures, this argument appears suspect. As long as the economy exhibits quantity-theoretic behavior, monetary aggregates represent a useful target for policymakers. Furthermore, in view of the destablizing posture of fiscal policy, use of quantitative targets gives the central bank the political advantage of being able to resist demands for greater accommodation of fiscal deficits. For the same reason, a return to pegging interest rates can be ruled out as likely to make monetary outcomes more dependent on fiscal impulses and therefore more destabilizing.

The Federal Reserve's disinflationary program of 1979-1982 has received much criticism for adhering to targets for a single monetary aggregate, but this argument may already be obsolete. Over the last two years the Federal Reserve has moved in the direction of a multiple target system. Quantitative ranges have been set for the major aggregates and the monetary base. At the same time, the Federal Reserve appears to have adopted implicit targets, or at least assumptions, for the nominal GNP. A system of multiple targets incorporating nominal income as well as monetary aggregates and bank reserves, offers the central bank adequate flexibility and is undoubtedly preferable to rigid adherence to a single indicator. Making explicit the assumptions for each indicator would help institutionalize the multiple target system.[37]

To some extent of course, the debate over operating targets is of secondary importance to the issue of where the targets are set. The cyclical fluctuations in the economy since 1979 were not so much the result of a transition to quantitative targets as the result of nine quarters of disinflation through mid-1982 followed by tolerance of above-target rates of monetary expansion. Over the long term, however, the question of the most appropriate stance for monetary policy has yet to be resolved. In the orthodox monetarist camp, the Federal Reserve has been faulted for failing to stabilize the short-term growth of the money supply. The monetarist constant growth rate principle, whereby targets for the growth of monetary aggregates are fixed and discretion eliminated, has itself been subject to increased criticism in the wake of the developments of 1979-1982, however. If the adjustment of wages and prices to monetary impulses is relatively gradual, fixed monetary targeting may accentuate the losses in output and employment associated with disinflation. Long-term inertia in wage-price equilibration and asymmetric rigidities theoretically could deflect the growth path of the economy below its potential permanently. A more recent type of critique concerns changes in the definitions of monetary aggregates and the decoupling of the money-income relationship implied by fluc-

109

tuations in velocity. Given the velocity decline in 1982, a fixed target policy would have accentuated cyclical output losses. Evidence associated with the New Federal Reserve Policy does not support the case for a constant monetary growth rule but instead suggests that it would be destabilizing.

There may be merit in allowing greater countercyclical variations in monetary aggregates while retaining use of quantitative ranges. Under a countercyclical system, annual ranges would be readjusted in light of slack in the economy or the rate of inflation. The Federal Reserve would be able to "lean against" the business cycle more effectively than under a fixed growth rate rule. Moreover, deviations from target ranges would be allowed to offset velocity fluctuations. Given an economy characterized by inertia in market equilibration and cyclical variations in velocity, a countercyclical monetary rule in which the central bank is able to react to the state of the economy would ultimately prove more stabilizing than a fixed growth rate rule in which cyclical changes in economic activity are necessarily ignored.[37]

Although macroeconomic policy has been guided primarily by domestic stabilization goals, there have been suggestions by political leaders of Western Europe, among others, that macroeconomic policy should pay greater attention to the dollar exchange rate and the growth of international liquidity. In view of the dollar's status as a reserve currency and the implications of exchange rate fluctuations for the global economy, explicit targets for the dollar would probably enhance the stability of the international economy. Under such a system, the exchange rate would be allowed to float within a given target range; minor deviations from the range could be corrected through purchases and sales of dollars in foreign exchange markets. The use of foreign currency operations, however, is relatively powerless to affect the fundamental determinants of exchange rates. Consequently, macroeconomic policies would have to be brought into greater alignment with those abroad to achieve an exchange rate target. This option presumes more extensive multilateral cooperation than has existed since the end of Bretton Woods. Given the current overvaluation of the exchange rate, moreover, a policy aimed at lowering the dollar to levels more closely approximating purchasing power parity would require faster monetary expansion. Consequently, restoring external competitiveness could only be achieved at the expense of an acceleration in inflation, even if accompanied by greater fiscal restraint. In short, making macroeconomic policy subordinate to an external target would require substantial trade-offs in other areas and would in all likelihood be politically unfeasible.

110

In fiscal policy there is at once a general consensus on the importance of deficit reduction but little agreement as to which fiscal indicators should be targeted. The Reagan administration's premise that conventional Keynesian theory of fiscal stabilization was obsolete appears to have been premature at best. From the standpoint of achieving a less asymmetric mix of monetary and fiscal policy, there may be merit in resurrecting such measures as the high employment budget as the basis for fiscal policy. Under a high employment surplus rule, deficits would be incurred primarily during recessionary periods, while surpluses would reduce inflationary pressures during periods of high employment. There is, of course, nothing novel about this idea, but there is also little doubt that a consistently implemented high employment surplus rule would be more stabilizing than the fiscal policies in force since the late 1960s and far preferable to a balanced budget rule established by constitutional fiat. Attempts to enforce an annual balanced budget would generate vicious cycles of fiscal restriction and declining economic activity as occurred in the 1930s when attempts to enforce balanced budgets through tax increases accelerated the speed of contraction. Furthermore, countries that have adhered to fiscal equilibrium policies during the postwar era such as France and Switzerland have normally allowed countercyclical deficits during recessions.

Unquestionably, a high employment surplus rule would be more stabilizing in the long run than the structural deficits projected under current policy. By the same token, a more restrictive fiscal posture would be preferable to the current over-expansionary stance. Nevertheless, major obstacles stand in the way of enforcement of greater fiscal restraint. Current projections of a nominal deficit of roughly 4 percent of the GNP though the end of the decade may turn out to be optimistic, because a recession at any time in the next three years would imply cyclical increases in federal borrowing requirements. Moreover, the fiscal compromises being discussed do not resolve the issue of structural deficits. Reducing the structural deficit would require politically difficult choices regarding the allocation of resources to defense and income transfers as well as levels of taxation. It is by no means clear that the political system will be capable of making these decisions and avoiding deadlock. The most politically likely scenario projected for after the 1984 election, one of a second term for the Reagan administration with a more heavily Democratic Congress, could therefore ultimately resolve itself as a period of political stagnation with fiscal policy left more or less on its present course.

Conclusions

The economic outlook for the remainder of the 1980s is fundamentally dependent on the macroeconomic policy mix. A continuation of current monetary policies implies less cyclical instability during the 1980s than the United States experienced in the previous decade. The growth rate during recoveries will probably be lower than its postwar trend, but the acceleration in inflation also will be less marked. Recessions should therefore be milder, barring a third oil shock or an international financial crisis sparked by widespread LDC debt defaults.

A continuation of structural fiscal deficits implies higher than average nominal and real interest rates over the business cycle and slower growth rates in credit-sensitive industries. Although current trade deficits imply some downward movement in the dollar, a long-term real interest rate differential between the United States and the other industrial countries would tend to hold the exchange rate permanently above purchasing power parity. The result would be a long-term loss in U.S. competitiveness, similar to that of the Bretton Woods period, and slower growth worldwide. A shift to a more restrictive fiscal policy aimed at gradually bringing the high employment deficit into equilibrium, or at least reducing the current fiscal-monetary asymmetry, would substantially improve the long-term outlook. Nevertheless, the mustering of political will necessary to accomplish this turnaround is, at best, a remote prospect.

Notes

1. Robert Z. Lawrence, *Can America Compete?* (Washington, D.C.: The Brookings Institution, 1984).

2. On the productivity slowdown, see in particular the following: Martin N. Bailey, "Productivity and the Services of Capital and Labor" in *Brookings Papers on Economic Activity*, no. 1 (1981), 1-50; Martin N. Bailey, "The Productivity Slowdown by Industry," in *Brookings Papers on Economic Activity*, no. 2 (1982), 423-454; Michael Bruno, "World Shock, Macroeconomic Response, and the Productivity Puzzle," National Bureau of Economic Research working paper no. 942 (1982); Gregory Christainsen and Robert Haveman, "Public Regulations and the Slowdown in Productivity Growth," in *American Economic Review*, vol. 71, no. 2 (1981), 320-325; Otto Eckstein and Robert Tannenwald, "Productivity and Capital Formation," in *Data Resources Review of the U.S. Economy* (February 1981); Robert J. Gordon, "The 'End of Expansion' Phenomenon in Short-Run Productivity Behavior" in *Brookings Papers on Economic Activity*, no. 2 (1979), 447-461; John F. Helliwell, "Stagflation and the Productivity Slowdown in Canada, 1974-1982," National Bureau of Economic Research working paper no. 1185 (1983); Assar

Lindbeck, "The Recent Slowdown in Productivity Growth" in *Economic Journal*, vol. 93, no. 1 (1983), 13-34.

3. See on this issue Zvi Griliches, "R&D and the Productivity Slowdown" in *American Economic Review*, vol. 70, no. 2 (1980), 343-348.

4. See for instance Otto Eckstein et al., *The DRI Report on U.S. Manufacturing Industries* (Data Resources, Inc., 1984).

5. On this issue see John Hein, "The Dollar and U.S. Exports," Conference Board paper no. 158 (1984).

6. For a survey of recent developments in exchange rate theory, see Ann O. Krueger, *Exchange Rate Determination* (New York: Cambridge University Press, 1984).

7. The issue of the complementarity of factor inputs of capital and energy has recently received greater attention in the literature on production functions, and some recent studies have suggested that energy and capital should be subaggregated into a single term rather than entered into the equation separately. See in this respect Yacov Sheinin, "The Four Factor Production Function Under The Three-Level CES Production Function," unpublished doctoral dissertion, University of Pennsylvania, Economics Department (1980).

8. On the issue of accommodation of oil shocks by monetary policy, see Phillip Cagan, "Imported Inflation, 1973-1974, and the Accommodation Issue," National Bureau of Economic Research working paper no. 258 (1978); Robert J. Gordon, "Alternative Responses of Policy to External Supply Shocks" in *Brookings Papers on Economic Activity*, no. 1 (1975), 183-206; Stanley Fischer, "Supply Shocks, Wage Stickiness and Accommodation," National Bureau of Economic Research working paper no. 1119 (May 1983); Edmund Phelps, "Commodity-Supply Shocks and Full Employment Monetary Policy" in *Journal of Money, Credit and Banking*, vol. 10, no. 2, pp. 206-221.

9. Katherine Abraham, "Structural/Frictional Versus Deficient Demand Unemployment" in *American Economic Review*, vol. 84, no. 4, (1983), 708-724.

10. For a discussion of macroeconomic policy during the 1960s and its implications for inflation see in particular Otto Eckstein and Roger Brinner, "The Inflation Process in the United States," study prepared for the Joint Economic Committee (Washington, D.C.: U.S. Government Printing Office, 1982).

11. The idea of an election year cycle, or "political business cycle," was originally proposed in William Nordhaus, "The Political Business Cycle" in *Review of Economic Studies*, vol. 42, no. 1 (1975), 169-190.

12. For estimates of the effects of the controls on the price level, see Alan S. Blinder and William Newton, "The 1971-74 Controls

Program and the Price Level: An Econometric Post-Mortem," National Bureau of Economic Research working paper no. 279 (1978).

13. See in this respect Robert J. Gordon, "Wage-Price Controls and the Shifting Phillips Curve" in *Brookings Papers on Economic Activity*, no. 2 (1972), 385-421; and Robert J. Gordon, "The Response of Wages and Prices to the First Two Years of Controls" in *Brookings Papers on Economic Activity*, no. 3 (1973), 765-780.

14. There has been a major debate in economic theory over the extent to which reserve flows can be sterilized through offsetting movements in domestic credit. On the issue see in particular Maurice Obstfeld, "Can We Sterilize: Theory and Evidence," National Bureau of Economic Research working paper no. 833 (1982).

15. This conclusion is reached in the report of the McCracken Commission, which conducted an in-depth study of this period. See Paul McCracken et al., *Towards Full Employment and Price Stability*, (Paris: OECD, 1978).

16. The removal of wage-price controls in 1974 is estimated by Blinder and Newton to have raised the price level by a full percentage point above its free market level. Similar results are obtained in Otto Eckstein, *The Great Recession*, (New York: Elsevier-North Holland, 1978). Other studies have argued that this estimate confuses the wage-price rebound with other factors such as the depreciation of the dollar. See on this point Robert J. Gordon and Jon Frye, "The Variance and Acceleration of Inflation in the 1970s," National Bureau of Economic Research working paper no. 551 (1980).

17. On this period, see Otto Eckstein, *The Great Recession*. Econometric simulations suggest that in the absence of the fiscal stimulus, the output losses during the 1974-1975 recession would have been considerably greater and the cyclical recovery in 1975-1976 correspondingly weaker.

18. In West Germany and Japan this was achieved successfully, albeit at the cost of substantially slower growth rates and losses in competitiveness due to appreciating exchange rates. The inflation rate, however, remained stable or decelerated until mid-1979 in both countries.

19. To some degree policymakers may have been misled by the lower reported values of the money supply in 1976-1978, which were subsequently revised upward. The original computed growth rates for M1 were 5.8 percent in 1976, 7.9 percent in 1977, 7.2 percent in 1978, and 5.5 percent in 1979. These growth rates were consistently lower than predicted monetary growth rates based on the demand for money at this time. As a result of the tendency of M1 to fall below its predicted

level, a decline in the demand for money and an increase in monetary velocity are hypothesized to have occurred during the late 1970s. See in this respect David Laidler, "The Demand for Money in the United States-Yet Again" in Karl Brunner and Allan Meltzer, eds., *On the State of Macroeconomics*, Carnegie-Rochester Conference Series on Public Policy, vol 12. (New York: Elsevier-North Holland, 1980).

20. In 1979, capacity utilization in Japan was only 80.2 percent. The industrial operating ratios for other major countries were also well below the levels of utilization attained during the late 1960s and 1971-1973.

21. On this point see Robert J. Gordon, "Inflation, Flexible Exchange Rates, and the Natural Rate of Unemployment" in Martin N. Bailey, ed., *Workers, Jobs and Inflation* (Washington, D.C.: Brookings Institution, 1982).

22. Robert J. Gordon, "Inflation, Flexible Exchange Rates, and the Natural Rate of Unemployment."

23. See in this respect Jeffrey M. Perloff and Michael Wachter, "A Production Function-Nonaccelerating Inflation Approach to Potential Output: Is Measured Potential Output Too High?" in Karl Brunner and Allan Meltzer, eds. *Three Aspects of Policy and Policymaking*, Carnegie-Rochester Conference Series on Public Policy, vol. 10 (New York: Elsevier-North Holland, 1979).

24. Alan S. Blinder, "Retail Inventory Behavior and Business Fluctuations" in *Brookings Papers on Economic Activity*, no. 2 (1981), 443-505.

25. In 1981 the target range for the redefined narrow monetary aggregate, shift-adjusted M1-B, was 3.5 percent to 6.0 percent, while the target for nominal M1-B was 6.0 percent to 8.5 percent. Over the 12 month period, shift-adjusted M1-B grew by 2.3 percent and nominal M1-B grew by 5.0 percent, in each case below the lower limit of the target range. In the first quarter of 1982, M1 (now returning to its old designation) increased by over 10 percent, but this was offset by a decline in velocity, resulting in a net decline in nominal GNP. During the second quarter, M1 was brought back within its target range.

26. The Third World debt crisis emerged in 1981 as a result of a series of factors. The appreciation of the dollar in 1981 raised the real cost of LDC debt, much of which was dollar-denominated; the rise in interest rates in the United States had a similar effect. Simultaneously, the slowdown in monetary growth in the United States entailed a diminution of reserve flows to the LDCs, while the global recession lowered demand for LDC exports and created critical shortages of

foreign exchange. Given the threat of widespread LDC debt defaults, the Federal Reserve's loosening actions in 1982 were motivated by the need to reduce interest rates on dollar loans and to raise the global supply of dollar liquidity. For a more detailed discussion of the Third World debt issues, see International Monetary Fund, *World Economic Outlook* (Washington, D.C.: IMF, 1983 and 1984).

27. Allen Sinai, Andrew Lin, and Russel Robins, "Taxes Savings and Investment: Some Empirical Evidence," in *National Tax Journal*, vol. 36, no. 3 (1983), 321-345.

28. There has been considerable debate over the relative contribution of shifts from other aggregates in the explosion of M1 at this time. See in this respect the following: James Johannes and Robert Rasche, "Forecasting Multipliers for the New Monetary Aggregates," Center for Research in Government, Policy and Business (University of Rochester, 1981); R.W. Hafer, "The Money-GNP Link: Assessing Alternative Transactions Measures" in *Federal Reserve Bank of St. Louis Review*, vol. 66, no. 3 (1984), 19-27; John Tatom, "Recent Financial Innovations: Have They Distorted the Meaning of M1?" in *Federal Reserve Bank of St. Louis Review*, vol. 64, no. 2, pp. 23-35.

29. On the determinants of the behavior of inventories in this period, see M.A. Akhtar, "Effects of Interest Rates and Inflation on Aggregate Inventory Investment in the United States" in *American Economic Review*, vol. 73, no. 3 (1983), 319-328.

30. Baseline projections by the Congressional Budget Office developed in early 1984 show the unified budget deficit reaching 5.6 percent of GNP in 1988, when the standardized employment deficit reaches 4.9 percent of the GNP. The baseline projections, however, allow for no changes in current policy. For alternative projections see Congressional Budget Office, "Baseline Budget Projections for Fiscal Years 1985-1989," (Washington, D.C.: U.S. Government Printing Office, 1984).

31. For tests of the growth of the public sector in the industrial countries as a whole, see David Cameron, "The Expansion of the Public Economy: A Comparative Analysis," in *American Political Science Review*, vol. 72, no. 4 (1978), 1242-1262. For tests limited to the United States, see David Lowery and William Berry, "The Growth of Government in the United States: An Empirical Assessment of Competing Explanations" in *American Journal of Political Science*, vol. 27, no. 4, (1982), 665-694.

32. The Reagan administration originally projected a deficit of $54 billion in FY 1981, declining sharply over the next three years and moving into surplus by FY 1984. The scenario assumed real GNP

growth of 4.2 percent in 1982, 5.0 percent in 1983, and 4.5 percent in 1984. These projections were made in the White House's "America's New Beginning: A Program For Economic Recovery," (Washington, D.C.: Office of the Press Secretary, 1981).

33. See for instance Michael D. Levy, "Factors Affecting Monetary Policy in an Era of Inflation" in *Journal of Monetary Economics*, vol. 8, no. 3 (1981), 351-373.

34. On this issue, see in particular Alan S. Blinder, "Issues in the Coordination of Monetary and Fiscal Policy," National Bureau of Economic Research working paper no. 982 (1982), and Alan S. Blinder, "On the Monetization of Fiscal Deficits," National Bureau of Economic Research working paper no. 1052 (1982). See also Robert J. Barro, "Comments From An Unreconstructed Richardian" in *Journal of Monetary Economics*, vol. 4, no. 3 (1978), 564-581; and William Niskanen, "Deficits, Government Spending and Inflation: What is the Evidence?" in *Journal of Monetary Economics*, vol. 4, no. 3, pp. 591-602.

35. See Douglas Hibbs, "Political Parties and Macroeconomic Policy" in *American Political Science Review*, vol. 71, no. 4 (1977), 705-731. For additional references, see James Alt and R. Alec Chystal, *Political Economics* (Berkeley and Los Angeles: University of California Press, 1983).

36. For a more extensive discussion see the debates on fiscal and monetary policy in *American Economic Review*, vol. 74, no. 2 (1984) and in particular the following pieces: Robert Eisner, "Which Budget Deficit? Some Issues of Measurement and Their Implications," 138-143; Benjamin Friedman, "Lessons from the 1979-82 Monetary Policy Experiment," 382-387; Bennett McCallum, "Monetarist Rules in the Light of Recent Experience," 388-391; James L. Pierce, "Did Financial Innovations Hurt the Great Monetarist Experiment?" 392-396.

37. Multiple target systems have been used systematically throughout most of the other major industrial countries. For descriptions of central bank operating procedures abroad, see OECD, *Monetary Targets and Inflation Control* (Paris: OECD, 1979).

38. On this issue see Stanley Fischer and J. Phillip Cooper, "Stabilization Policy and Lags" in *Journal of Political Economy*, vol. 81, no. 3 (1973), 847-887; John B. Taylor, "Estimation and Control of a Macroeconomic Model with Rational Expectations" in *Econometrica*, vol. 47, no. 3 (1979), 1267-1286; John B. Taylor, "Stabilization, Accommodation, and Monetary Rules" in *American Economic Review*, vol. 71, no. 2 (1981), 145-149.

THE QUADRANGULAR FORUM
WORKING GROUPS

■■■■■■■■■■■■■■■■

United States Working Group

Chairman:

WILLIAM E. BROCK
U.S. Trade Representative

PAUL A. ALLAIRE
Xerox Corporation

ROBERT ANDERSON
Rockwell International Corporation

STANTON D. ANDERSON
Anderson, Hibey, Nauheim & Blair

LLOYD BENTSEN
U.S. Senate

JAMES F. BERE
Borg-Warner Corporation

C. FRED BERGSTEN
Institute for International Economics

DON BONKER
U.S. House of Representatives

BILL BRADLEY
U.S. Senate

LEO CHERNE
Research Institute of America

JACK CLARKE
Exxon Corporation

DOUGLAS D. DANFORTH
Westinghouse Electric Co.

JOHN C. DANFORTH
U.S. Senate

WILLIAM DRAPER
The Export-Import Bank

GEZA FEKETEKUTY
Office of the United States
  Trade Representative

MURRAY FINLEY
Amalgamated Clothing &
  Textile Workers Union

PETER FLANIGAN
Dillon, Read & Co.

JAMES FRIERSON
Office of the United States
  Trade Representative

ROBERT GALVIN
Motorola, Inc.

J. LESLIE GLICK
Genex Corporation

MAURICE R. GREENBERG
American International Group, Inc.

PENELOPE HARTLAND-THUNBERG
CSIS

WILLIAM HOLLAND
Coopers & Lybrand

ROBERT HORMATS
Goldman, Sachs & Co.

LEE A. IACOCCA
Chrysler Corporation

B. R. INMAN
Microelectronics and Technology
  Corporation

AMOS A. JORDAN
CSIS

ROBERT H. KRIEBLE
Loctite Corporation

THOMAS G. LABRECQUE
The Chase Manhattan Bank, N.A.

JAMES E. LEE
Gulf Oil Corporation

ROBERT LUNDEEN
Dow Chemical

R. TIMOTHY MCNAMAR
Department of the Treasury

HARALD B. MALMGREN
Malmgren, Inc.

ROBERT H. MALOTT
FMC Corporation

JOHN C. MAROUS, JR.
Westinghouse Electric Co.

LIONEL OLMER
Department of Commerce

WILLIAM V. ROTH, JR.
U.S. Senate

MICHAEL SAMUELS
U.S. Chamber of Commerce

NATHANIEL SAMUELS
Lehman Brothers Kuhn Loeb, Inc.

G. HENRY M. SCHULER
CSIS

CHARLES E. SCHUMER
U.S. House of Representatives

WALLACE O. SELLERS
Merrill Lynch & Co.

MARK SHEPHERD, JR.
Texas Instruments, Inc.

FRANCIS STANKARD
The Chase Manhattan Bank, N.A.

HERBERT STEIN
American Enterprise Institute

PAULA STERN
U.S. International Trade
    Commission

ROBERT STRAUSS
Akin, Gump, Strauss, Hauer
    & Feld

THOMAS C. THEOBALD
Citibank N.A.

WILLIAM E. TIMMONS
Timmons & Co.

ALEXANDER TOMLINSON
National Planning Association

GEORGE VOJTA
Deak-Perera

HENRY C. WALLICH
Federal Reserve System

W. ALLEN WALLIS
Department of State

SHELDON WEINIG
Materials Research Corporation

MARINA V.N. WHITMAN
General Motors Corporation

T. A. WILSON
The Boeing Company

CLAYTON YEUTTER
Chicago Mercantile Exchange

JOHN YOCHELSON
CSIS

Japanese Working Group

Chairman:
SABURO OKITA
Institute for International &
    Domestic Policy Studies

Cochairmen:
SHOICHIRO TOYODA
Toyota Motor Corporation

ICHIRO HATTORI
Daini Seikosha

YASUO TAKEYAMA
Nihon Keizai Shimbun

SHOICHI AKAZAWA
Fujitsu

YOSHITOKI CHINO
Daiwa Securities

GAISHI HIRAIWA
Tokyo Electric Power

TAKASHI HOSOMI
Overseas Economic Cooperation Fund

CHIHIRO HOSOYA
Hitotsubashi University

120

MASAMICHI INOKI
Research Institute for Peace
and Security

HIROSHI INOSE
The University of Tokyo

ROKURO ISHIKAWA
Kajima Corporation

KENICHI ITO
CSIS Tokyo Representative

MASAO KAMEI
Sumitomo Electric Industries

YOTARO KOBAYASHI
Fuji Xerox

ISAMU MIYAZAKI
Daiwa Securities Research
Institute

MASAYA MIYOSHI
Federation of Economic
Organizations

YUZABURO MOGI
Kikkoman Corporation

NOBUYUKI NAKAHARA
Toa Nenryo Kogyo

MASASHI NISHIHARA
National Defense Academy

KIICHI SAEKI
Nomura Research Institute

KEIZO SAJI
Suntory

SEIZABURO SATO
The University of Tokyo

YUTAKA TAKEDA
Nippon Steel Corporation

KEIYA TOYONAGA
Sumitomo Bank

AKIYOSHI WADA
The University of Tokyo

YASUSHI WATANABE
Bank of Tokyo

ISAMU YAMASHITA
Mitsui Shipbuilding and
Engineering

BUNROKU YOSHINO
Federation of Economic
Organizations

European Working Group

Cochairmen:

ETIENNE DAVIGNON
Commission of the European Communities

GERRIT A. WAGNER
Royal Dutch Petroleum
Netherlands

UMBERTO AGNELLI
Fiat S.P.A.
Italy

HUBERT CARNIAUX
The Group of Presidents
Belgium

FRANCOIS DANIS
The Spaak Foundation
Belgium

W. DEKKER
Phillips Gloeilampenfabrieken
Netherlands

JEAN FRANCOIS-PONCET
Former Foreign Minister
France

JEAN GODEAUX
National Bank of Belgium
Belgium

MAURICE HODGSON
British Home Stores
Great Britain

JOSE RAMON LASUEN
University of Madrid
Spain

ARNAUD LEENHARDT
Societe Vallourec
France

121

H.O. THIERBACH
Deutsche Bank
Federal Republic of Germany

SIMONE VEIL
Member of the European Parliament
France

EBERHARD VON KUENHEIM
BMW
Federal Republic of Germany

Canadian Working Group

Cochairmen:

EDWARD LUMLEY
Minister of Industry

CEDRIC RITCHIE
Bank of Nova Scotia

LAURENT BEAUDOIN
Bombadier Inc.

JOHN BRAGG
Oxford Frozen Food Ltd.

SHIRLEY CARR
Canadian Labour Congress

JOHN CURTIS
Institute for Policy Research

PAUL DESMARAIS
Power Corporation of Canada

BRUCE HOWE
British Columbia Resources
    Investment Corporation

T. MAXWELL
Conference Board of Canada

G.E.M. NEWELL
Dupont Canada, Inc.

J.H. STEVENS
Canada Wire and Cable Limited

ROBERT WHITE
United Auto Workers

CSIS SECRETARIAT

Director of the Quadrangular Forum

JOHN YOCHELSON
Director of CSIS International Business
and Economics Program

Quadrangular Forum Advisors

PENELOPE HARTLAND-THUNBERG
Holder of the William M. Scholl Chair
in International Business, CSIS

STEPHEN A. MERRILL
Fellow
CSIS International Business
and Economics Program

Quadrangular Forum Coordinator

CATHERINE STIRLING
Research Associate
CSIS International Business and Economics Program

Overseas Liaison

JOHN CURTIS
Director, Institute for Policy Research
Canada

KENICHI ITO
CSIS Tokyo Representative
Japan

PETER LUDLOW
Director, Centre for
European Policy Studies